LILY HOWARD

FOREWORD BY GEORG

# THE WORDS THAT SHAPE US

The Science-Based Power of Teacher Language

**SCHOLASTIC**

\* Some of the names of real individuals have been changed to protect their confidentiality. In all other cases, real names have been used.

Excepting those parts intended for classroom use, no part of this publication may be reproduced in whole or in part, or stored in a retrieval system, or transmitted in any form or by any means, electronic, mechanical, photocopying, recording, or otherwise, or used to train any artificial intelligence technologies, without the express written permission of the publisher. For information regarding permission, write to Scholastic Inc., 557 Broadway, New York, NY 10012. Scholastic Inc. grants teachers who have purchased this product permission to reproduce from this book those pages intended for use in their classrooms. Notice of copyright must appear on all copies of copyrighted materials.

SVP & Publisher: Tara Welty
Editor: Maria L. Chang
Cover design: Tannaz Fassihi
Interior design: Maria Lilja
Opening pages art: Tanya Chernyak
Interior images: Stock photos © Getty Images, Shutterstock.com and The Noun Project.
Images on pages 84–86 taken from THE CASE FOR LOVING by Selina Alko and Sean Qualls. Copyright © 2015 by Selina Alko and Sean Qualls. Reprinted by permission of Arthur A. Levine Books, an imprint of Scholastic Inc.

ISBN: 978-1-5461-3099-4

Scholastic Inc., 557 Broadway, New York, NY 10012
Copyright © 2025 by Lily Howard Scott
Published by Scholastic Inc. All rights reserved.
Printed in the U.S.A.
First printing, January 2025.

1 2 3 4 5 6 7 8 9 10    40    34 33 32 31 30 29 28 27 26 25

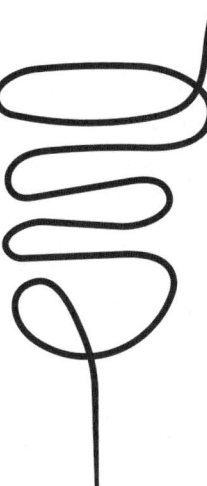

## DEDICATION

***To Conrad, Alexander, and Charlie***

There aren't words to wrap around my love for you, but:

"The inexpressible is contained—inexpressibly!—in the expressed."

(—Maggie Nelson, on Wittgenstein)

# Table of Contents

Foreword ............................................................................................................. 9

Introduction ...................................................................................................... 11

**PART 1** *Establish and Maintain a Connected Classroom Community* ............ 19

**BRAIN-CHANGING WORDS:** *"Everything you bring to our classroom community matters. What is something you'd like us to know about you?"*
*"Something I'd like you to know about me is ___."* ........................................ 21

Introducing This Language .............................................................................. 22

Kids' Turn ......................................................................................................... 23

Curricular Connections

    Poetry Invitation: Things to Know About Me/Us ...................................... 23

    Student-as-Teacher Initiative: "Something I bring
    to this classroom community is ___." ........................................................ 25

Partnering With Families ................................................................................. 26

**BRAIN-CHANGING WORDS:** *"We all have outer shells and inner swirls."*
*"Just because ___ doesn't mean ___."* .......................................................... 28

Introducing This Language .............................................................................. 29

Kids' Turn ......................................................................................................... 32

Curricular Connections

    Character Map: Outer Shell/Inner Swirls ................................................... 34

    Reading Response: Noticing and Interrupting Assumptions .................... 35

    Poetry Invitation: Just Because .................................................................. 36

Partnering With Families ................................................................................. 37

**BRAIN-CHANGING WORDS:** *"What are the windows and mirrors within our classroom community?"* ............................................................................ 39

Introducing This Language .............................................................................. 41

Kids' Turn ......................................................................................................... 42

Curricular Connections

    Individual Reflection Exercise: What Mirrors Are You Itching For? ......... 44

    Reading Response: Window/Mirror Jots and Silent Conversation .......... 45

Partnering With Families ................................................................................. 46

**BRAIN-CHANGING WORDS:** *"I love how/I felt/I never knew ___."* ................. 47

Introducing This Language ................................................................. 48

Kids' Turn ........................................................................................ 49

Curricular Connection

    Tribute Exchange: Important Thing ........................................... 53

Partnering With Families .................................................................. 55

## PART 2  *Cultivate Students' Self-Awareness, Self-Compassion, and Self-Regulation* ............ 56

**BRAIN-CHANGING WORDS:** *"Hello, feeling visitor!" "You are separate from your feeling."* ........................... 59

Introducing This Language ................................................................. 60

Kids' Turn ........................................................................................ 62

Curricular Connections

    Reading Response: Big Event → Feeling Visitor .......................... 63

    Poetry Invitation: Feeling Visitors Inside Me ................................ 64

Partnering With Families .................................................................. 66

**BRAIN-CHANGING WORDS:** *"What can your wisest self say back to other thoughts and feelings in your head?"* .......... 68

Introducing This Language ................................................................. 69

Kids' Turn ........................................................................................ 71

Curricular Connections

    Reading Response: Coaching Characters ..................................... 72

    Poetry Invitation: Listening to My Wisest Self ............................... 73

Partnering With Families .................................................................. 73

**BRAIN-CHANGING WORDS:** *"Turn on your 'birder mindset': What will you notice?"* ..... 75

Introducing This Language ................................................................. 76

Kids' Turn ........................................................................................ 78

Curricular Connections

    Take-Home Pocket Notebooks: What Will You Notice? ................. 79

    Reading Response: Read Like a Birder: Celebrating Craft Jots ...... 80

    Poetry Invitation: Birder Mindset ................................................. 81

Partnering With Families .................................................................. 81

**BRAIN-CHANGING WORDS: *"I spotlight you!"*** ..... 82
Introducing This Language ..... 83
Kids' Turn ..... 85
Curricular Connection
    **Reading Response: Spotlighting Picture Books and Photographs** ..... 86
Partnering With Families ..... 87

## PART 3 *Inspire Students to Strive for Independence and Take Academic Risks* ..... 88

**BRAIN-CHANGING WORDS: *"What a brilliant mistake!"*** ..... 90
Introducing This Language ..... 91
Kids' Turn ..... 92
Curricular Connection
    **Collaborative Nonfiction Text: Brilliant Mistakes Throughout History** ..... 93
Partnering With Families ..... 94

**BRAIN-CHANGING WORDS: *"Let's approach our work today—and every day— with an 'ishful' spirit."*** ..... 95
Introducing This Language ..... 95
Kids' Turn ..... 97
Curricular Connection
    **Free-Writes: Ishfully Dream Ideas Into Being** ..... 98
Partnering With Families ..... 98

**BRAIN-CHANGING WORDS: *"Just take it bird by bird and do the next small right thing."*** ..... 99
Introducing This Language ..... 99
Kids' Turn ..... 100
Curricular Connection
    **Poetry Invitation: Break It Down, Bird by Bird** ..... 101
Partnering With Families ..... 102

## PART 4  *Support Students When They Exhibit Challenging Behavior* ........ 103

**BRAIN-CHANGING WORDS:** *"You are always good inside even when you do not make a good choice."* .......... 105

Introducing This Language .......... 106

Kids' Turn .......... 107

Curricular Connections

    **Reading Response: Beyond Traits** .......... 107

    **Teacher Resource: Keep-Your-Cool Strategies and Language for End-of-Rope Moments** .......... 108

Partnering With Families .......... 109

**BRAIN-CHANGING WORDS:** *"Different things are hard for different people. What about ____ feels hard for you/me?"* .......... 111

Introducing This Language .......... 113

Kids' Turn .......... 114

Curricular Connection

    **Reading Response: Beneath Character Behavior: What's Hard for ___?** .......... 115

Partnering With Families .......... 116

**BRAIN-CHANGING WORDS:** *"Both/And"*
*"Intent/Impact"* .......... 117

Introducing This Language .......... 118

Kids' Turn .......... 119

Curricular Connections

    **Reading Response: Character Intent vs. Character Impact** .......... 120

    **Poetry Invitation: Many Sides of Me** .......... 120

Partnering With Families .......... 121

Conclusion .......... 122

Acknowledgments .......... 124

References .......... 126

Appendix: Reproducible Templates .......... 129

# Foreword
## by Georgia Heard

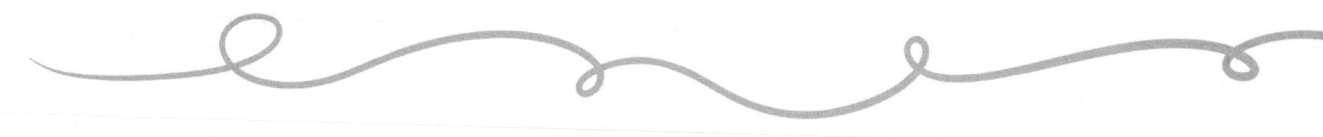

As a writer and teacher, I'm continually inspired by the astonishing power of language and its ability to shape our thoughts, emotions, and connections. As a parent, I only wish Lily Howard Scott's *The Words That Shape Us: The Science-Based Power of Teacher Language* had been available when I was raising my son and when he was in school. As I savored every word in this important book, I became more deeply aware of how small shifts in the language we use with children can create meaningful changes in the way they perceive themselves and help them navigate their inner worlds.

Lily offers numerous examples of language we can use in both the classroom and at home to empower young learners. She shows how words can guide children to listen to their inner voice, enabling them to make choices that prioritize their well-being—personally as well as academically. She reminds us that every interaction with a child can be an opportunity to plant seeds of understanding and growth.

In a time when children's mental health is increasingly at risk, *The Words That Shape Us* provides a compassionate framework for nurturing self-compassion and resilience in our youngest learners. Amidst the complexities of our world where language and truth are often compromised by disinformation—and children are frequently exposed to disempowering messages on social media—Lily offers a clarity about the power of words and gives us specific strategies for making a positive difference in our children's lives.

The language we use with children can help them navigate their inner worlds.

What I particularly love is how each chapter includes practical curricular connections, templates, and writing invitations that guide students in internalizing language that leads to self-knowledge and self-compassion through poetry, other genres, visual maps, and mentor texts. Lily provides examples of self-talk anchor charts for situations when school work feels challenging or confusing, or when a child feels unsure. She encourages children to honor their "wisest self" in the choices they make. Each chapter also incorporates ways for educators to partner with families so these strategies can be reinforced at home.

*The Words That Shape Us* is not only a practical guide for educators, parents, and caregivers; it's a heartfelt invitation to cultivate a more supportive and caring environment for our children by becoming more attune to the language we use and guiding children in this awareness. This essential book encourages us all to embrace a simple yet profound understanding of how words can transform our classrooms, homes, and, ultimately, our world.

----

**Georgia Heard** is an internationally acclaimed poet and teacher of writing. She is the author of *Awakening the Heart*, *Heart Maps*, and *A Place for Wonder*, among many other books.

# Introduction

"The limits of my language mean the limits of my world."

—LUDWIG WITTGENSTEIN

When my son Alexander was 4, I optimistically introduced a new phrase to him: *inner voice*. A few of his preschool classmates had invented a "rhino ramming game" that centered around—you guessed it—ramming into each other like angry rhinoceroses. While I certainly understood the appeal, kids were getting hurt. We talked about how, though he'd likely feel tempted to join in the excitement next time, he had a choice: He could follow the group, or he could listen to his inner voice (the wisest, truest part of himself) and make the safe decision.

Alexander looked at me blankly. My words seemed to bounce off him. Then, grinning, he said, "Can I have a pet piranha one day if I promise never to touch it?"

I dropped the issue.

A few weeks later, while enjoying a book about medieval times, Alexander lingered on a section about jousting. I had just finished reading aloud a caption about the dangers of the sport: broken limbs, concussions, and some other sinister things I pretended weren't on the page. We stared at a gorgeous illustration of two knights mounted on plumed horses, lances ready, poised to gallop toward each other. Alexander pointed to one of the horses and softly said, "If I was a horse in medieval times and a knight was poking me with spurs so he could joust and hurt someone, I would listen to my inner voice and not move. I would just eat grass."

My throat tightened, and I nearly laughed out loud. The phrase *had* nestled inside of him. And it had led him to a new, surprisingly sophisticated understanding: Even when things are poised to go one way, even when you feel pressured toward an outcome that feels inevitable, there's always a second option. You can listen to yourself and change course. (In this case, you can take a stand as a defiant, pacifist horse.) I kissed the top of Alexander's head and thought: *Language is magic.* Linguist Noam Chomsky says that "language etches the grooves through which your thoughts must flow." And those two words—*inner voice*—had etched grooves that took my son's thinking somewhere wonderful, somewhere I hope he returns to over and over again as he navigates inevitable pressures and challenges ahead.

*The Words That Shape Us* is about the two big interests of my life: children and language. It's about how the words we use with kids can positively transform how they think, feel, and do. Just as the simple phrase *inner voice* helped my son understand that he could rely on his own internal compass, the language that teachers share with students can unlock their potential in the classroom, helping them become more confident, creative, resilient learners.

And that language can have far deeper and longer-lasting impacts, too. Pulitzer Prize–winning author Marilynne Robinson shared that the most valuable advice she ever received came from an English teacher, Ms. Soderling, who told her, "You will have to live with your mind every day of your life, so make sure you have a mind that you want to live with." It has never been more important to help children cultivate minds they want to live with: The American Academy of Pediatrics has declared children's mental health a national emergency (2021). This book explores how the words we share with children can help them develop kinder, more joyful minds; minds that point them toward self-trust and self-compassion; minds that are good company to live with.

The language teachers share with students can unlock their potential in the classroom.

# Language as a Brain-Changing Tool

Human language is ordinary from a distance and dizzying up close. By using a few dozen recurring symbols, we can extract infinite ideas from within ourselves and share them with others (a practice that, as far as we know, sets us apart from all other animals). Language has traditionally been considered in this conduit role: as the vehicle for the expression of thought, not its progenitor (Gleitman & Papafragou, 2012). But recently, I've become fascinated with the idea that language not only helps us express what's within—it *transforms* what's within.

Thanks to remarkable advances in science of emotion and neuroplasticity, we now know that words we hear and use every day can literally shape our brain, changing microscopic parts of our neurons and inviting us to create new mental concepts (Barrett, 2017). Neuroscientist Lisa Feldman Barrett teaches us: "Words seed your concepts, concepts drive your predictions, predictions regulate your body budget, and your body budget determines how you feel." This insight explains why the language we use to describe our emotions can actually shape our emotional perceptions and experiences themselves (Lindquist, et al., 2015). Having a nuanced emotional vocabulary and accurately labeling a complex or difficult feeling help us understand that the feeling is something we *experience*, not something we *are*. We can see the emotion from a distance and "name it to tame it," as Dr. Dan Siegel (Bryson & Siegel, 2012) puts it.

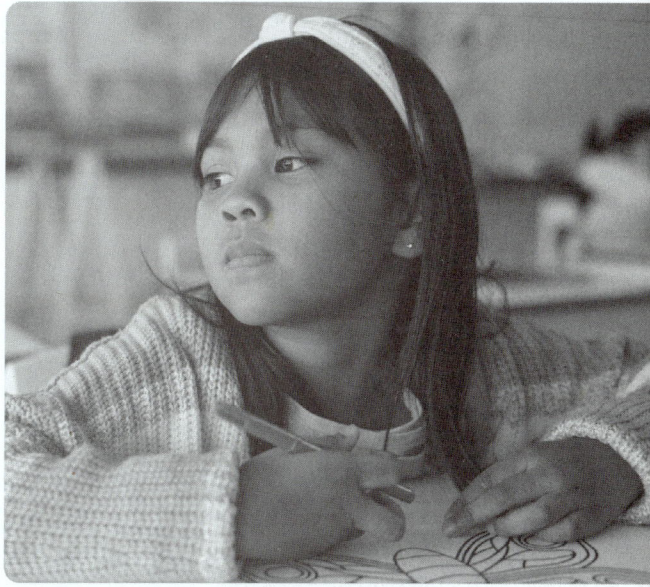

The words and phrases to which kids have access can trigger healthier patterns of thinking and behavior.

But it wasn't until I read Larissa MacFarquhar's *New Yorker* profile of cognitive scientist and philosopher Andy Clark that I had my "aha!" moment about language as the most powerful, practical tool available to me as a person, parent-to-be, and teacher. Of Clark, MacFarquhar (2018) writes:

> How is it that human thought is so deeply different from that of other animals, even though our brains can be quite similar? The difference is due, [Clark] believes, to our heightened ability to incorporate props and tools into our thinking, to use them to think thoughts we could never have otherwise. . . . Any human who uses language to think with has already incorporated an external device into his most intimate self, and the connections only proliferate from there.

Clark believes that most thinking happens in between our brains and whatever tool we're using. This is why, when sketching with a pencil, we often find ourselves drawing something completely different from what we'd initially planned when we contemplated our artwork with no utensil yet in hand. Spur-of-the-moment ideas come to us *because* we're using a pencil, which seems to lead the way. And this is why the words and phrases to which we have access trigger thoughts, feelings, and behavior only *because* of that particular language—that particular "tool."

Introduction

## Transformative Language in the Classroom

When I read about Clark's ideas, tools were on my mind. I was teaching third grade (alongside a wonderful co-teacher, Anneliese) in an integrated co-teaching (ICT) classroom at P.S. 321 in Brooklyn, New York. A third of our bright, endlessly creative students had individualized education plans (IEPs), and our classroom brimmed with a wide range of strengths and needs. Anneliese and I enjoyed dreaming up tools to help our students do their best: One child perched on a sensory cushion during circle time, another quietly sketched his mind movies while listening to read-alouds, and another benefited from extra movement breaks. Our classroom community was premised on the understanding that different kids need different things.

Early in the school year, however, we noticed that many students were navigating a shared struggle: shame around making mistakes. So we changed our language. When children made mistakes, instead of saying something like, "Don't worry, we all make mistakes; just try again!" we began calling these errors "brilliant mistakes."

We explained the neuroscience behind the importance of investigating mistakes: "Sitting with" mistakes leads to some of the most powerful cognitive growth of all (Dweck, 2007). And if paying attention to mistakes paves the way to brilliant new thinking—take, for example, Scottish scientist Alexander Fleming, who noticed the mold growing in a petri dish he left uncapped and ended up discovering penicillin—why not call mistakes "brilliant"? Our students listened, wide-eyed. At Anneliese's inspired suggestion, we erected a "Brilliant Mistake Wall" where the children jotted down or drew pictures of recent mistakes and noted their corresponding discoveries. When we asked who might be brave enough to display a brilliant mistake from a recent math assessment under the document camera and to share the specific learning that the error inspired, so many children clamored to be picked that we ended up celebrating (and learning from) mistake after mistake.

Students proudly share their mistakes—and what they learned from them—on the "Brilliant Mistake Wall."

Best of all, we watched the children tuck away this language and use it themselves, out loud and as self-talk. I heard one student, who was editing her writing, excitedly whisper to herself, "I found another brilliant mistake!" After quiet time one day, a child showed me his sketch of a castle and said, "I made a brilliant mistake, so I just decided to make the turret extra tall—which is cooler and safer for the archers, actually." As our students internalized this unusual phrase, errors that might have caused embarrassment or avoidance instead triggered self-compassion, curiosity, and, most crucially, a capacity to *keep going* when assignments got hard. (Learn more about how to incorporate this language in your classroom on page 90.)

How does such a simple phrase work its magic? In *How Emotions Are Made: The Secret Life of the Brain*, Lisa Feldman Barrett explains that emotions don't happen to us, they're *made* by us. They're "guesses" informed by previous experiences. This means we all have more agency over our interior lives than we might have realized. Deploying brilliant-mistake language is an example of a choice that Barrett calls an "energized determination": an approach that seeds our brains to predict differently in the future. When a child—let's say a first grader who typically shuts down emotionally when he spots mistakes—repeatedly relies on this language whenever he notices an error, the experience of catching slipups begins to feel viscerally different. Before long, miscalculations don't bother the student in the way they used to; he no longer feels sick to his stomach or paralyzed by self-consciousness because his brain has, quite literally, changed its response.

It has often been said, "I am as I am seen." Another way of thinking about this is: "I am as I hear you talk about me." We speak, a child hears us, tucks away our words, and revisits them later. This is both encouraging and alarming because it means our language really matters, in both wonderful and terrible ways. In *Hidden Gems,* writer and teacher Katherine Bomer emphasizes the power of teacher language by quoting poet Linda Hogan: "In so many ways we are creations of language, the things that people have said to us, the things they tell us we are." I like to think that years later, some of my former students still speak to themselves through this loving lens when they consider their mistakes and look for learning to carry forward.

> **Helping kids learn how to talk to themselves with love is a national imperative.**

Helping kids learn how to talk to themselves with love is a national imperative. Youth mental health is under unprecedented strain (APA, 2021). What does this emotional distress look like in schools? Every teacher I know has watched students hide under desks or scream at the top of their lungs. More subtly, we've seen children grip their pencils tightly as they feverishly complete an optional extra-credit assignment. Regulated anxiety masquerades as high achievement; dysregulated anxiety is usually diagnosed as a "behavior issue." Regardless of how it manifests, children are suffering, and they urgently need language to help them compassionately navigate their interior worlds.

Some believe that encouraging children to adopt a compassionate view of themselves is too "gentle" and can lead to distorted understandings of their strengths or areas for growth. Psychologist Susan David (2016) reminds us that nothing could be further from the truth: "Self-compassion is not about lying to yourself. In fact, it's the opposite. It's about looking at yourself from an outside perspective: a broad and inclusive view that doesn't deny reality but instead recognizes your challenges and failures as a part of being human."

Words are powerful tools for regulating minds and bodies, and the small moments between teachers and students *matter*. Change is rooted in the hundreds of tiny decisions we make each day and in the language we use throughout fleeting-yet-connected moments. Psychiatrist Bruce Perry (2021) teaches us that "the most powerful and enduring human interactions are often very brief." Educators don't need to abandon all the wonderful things they're already doing to transform their classroom culture and to give children powerful tools to positively manage their inner lives. Subtle changes in how we communicate can initiate a tectonic shift in how children perceive themselves, relate to others, and navigate challenges—in the classroom, at home, and beyond.

## How to Use This Book

This book is geared toward teachers of children in elementary school (broadly speaking, prekindergarten through fifth grade), though many of the language suggestions and strategies will resonate with younger and older children, too.

To me, being an elementary school teacher felt like being right in the center of human experience, surrounded by both luminous vulnerability and a hearty dose of screeching (sometimes joyful, sometimes distressed). Each school day was a seven-hour exercise in deep listening and improvisation, punctuated by moments that were deeply moving, hilarious, or surprising. No plan ever unfolded exactly how I imagined it would, and my brain often felt like it was on fire from making hundreds of split-second decisions. Halt the read-aloud because the kids won't stop looking at the hawk perched on the branch outside the window? Definitely. Chase after the child who bolted out of the classroom or holler down the hall for a colleague to intervene? Depends on whether or not my co-teacher happened to be in the room. And so forth.

When the children left at 3 PM, I created my own sensory-deprivation chamber. I turned off the overhead lights, ate leftover crackers in silence, and contemplated the next day. I reached for books that were inspiring and immediately useful to me; I was simply too wiped out to spend my energy translating abstract theory into practice. I loved Georgia Heard's *Heart Maps* because I could open it up to any page and photocopy a template of a heart map for the next day's morning work, or quickly create one of my own, inspired by what I saw. I didn't need to read the book from beginning to end to find something valuable. I could navigate it myself during this limited, precious alone time, using my experience and judgment to identify resources that I knew would work for my students.

At the end of the school day, I would reach for books that were inspiring and immediately useful to me.

This is what I hope to give you: a practical resource that feels like a comfort, an ally to sit with during your own post-dismissal quiet moment. This book is the opposite of a mandated curriculum. You can explore it according to your own priorities and needs, trying out language suggestions and curricular extensions in whatever order you like. For example, a fourth-grade teacher might pick up this book and walk away with language to use with a student who struggles to self-regulate, a peer-to-peer feedback protocol to try during a writing share the next morning, or a reading-response template to send along as homework.

I've organized this book into four parts, centered around the following goals:

1. **Establish and maintain a connected classroom community.**
2. **Cultivate students' self-awareness, self-compassion, and self-regulation.**
3. **Inspire students to strive for independence and take academic risks.**
4. **Support students when they exhibit challenging behavior.**

In each part, I include the following sections:

- **Language suggestions** and strategies for how children can use the words and phrases with one another and, when applicable, with themselves as self-talk.

- **Curricular connections** that empower students to internalize the language and apply it across subject areas. Poetry invitations abound in this section. Poet Mary Oliver (2021) once said that, unlike a chapter of a book, "people are more apt to remember a poem, and feel like they own it, and speak it to themselves." When kids write poetry centered around these language suggestions, the words are easier to remember and return to.

- **Partnering with families** by offering strategies for how parents and children can weave these phrases into their home lives and strategies for mining the riches of students' home languages and dialects. What bite-sized phrases and sayings can children bring back to the classroom?

About the recurring Partnering With Families section, when I refer to "parent," I include any trusted grown-up who supports the child at home, including a caregiver, grandparent, or another familiar person. When adults at school and at home use similar supportive language, especially in the context of challenging moments, the implications for kids are profound. Children feel enveloped by caring consistency and their associated learning is authentic, transferable, and—above all—practicable. Imagine a kindergartner who hears, "I spy a brilliant mistake; let's see what learning it holds!" at school *and* at home. This child has double the opportunities to internalize the language and to practice responding to errors with resilience and curiosity.

There are many ways to share the language suggestions with families: a newsletter, curriculum update, blog post, or parent-teacher conference. However you choose to share, it's important to pair your offering with an invitation for parents to adapt the language and offer suggestions of their own. I recall when my student Amelia shared a saying that her father, Dan, often repeated to her: "Most of the time, your problem is not your problem. Your response to your problem is your problem." Before I knew it, I found myself saying to students, "I see there's a problem. What happens next is up to you. How can you respond to what happened?" Eventually, kids started using this language themselves: "We both want the biggest paintbrush in the bin to paint the wagon. I'm going to respond by asking if there's a second big paintbrush in Ms. F's room. Can I go ask her?" Dan's words helped kids remember that they have agency in those first few moments after a problem pops up; instead of melting down, they can *do* something. And by thanking Dan for sharing this saying (which we displayed on our classroom wall) with us, I reinforced just how much language from home can enrich our classroom community, inspiring other children to keep an ear out for phrases they might bring in.

## Make It Your Own

The most important thing to know before diving into this book is that the language suggestions are exactly that: suggestions. They are not a script. Sometimes, it takes hearing another person's language to suddenly grasp the word you were searching for, the one that had been just out of reach.

A few years ago, I introduced the concept of an inner voice to my student Harper, then 8 years old. Harper suggested calling this wisest, truest part of herself her "President Decider" (see left) because, in her words, "President Decider is like the president of my body, and she gets to choose what to think about and what not to think about." Harper listened to her own genius (Muhammad, 2020) and found words that worked better for her. Effective teaching isn't about compliance; it's about what your contributions might stir up within the child, who in turn brings forth something new and wondrous of her own.

> **President Decider**
> By Harper and 3-306 Classmates
>
> **Pressure**
> You're the oldest.
> Stop playing right now.
> Do your challenge work.
>
> **President Decider**
> You don't always have to do your challenge work.
> It's good for you to play, too.
>
> **Worry**
> What if we lose all our money?
> You're spending too much money on books!
>
> **President Decider**
> Don't worry, you can always go to the library.
> Those books don't cost any money.

Harper explores what her inner voice—her "President Decider"—might say back to feelings of worry and pressure.

As you try on these nuggets of language, listen to yourself. How do the words feel? Do any adaptations spring to mind? I hope you'll lean into your own instincts. It's important that the words sit right with you as you introduce them to your students and appropriately-yet-vulnerably explore elements of your inner life. For instance, what might *your* inner voice—your president decider, or wisest self, or whatever you'd like to call this leader of your brain—say back to a feeling of self-doubt that visits you before you attempt something challenging?

We can't ask children to take risks unless we're brave enough to lead the way, not by sharing our deepest fears or by crossing a professional line, but simply by sharing something true. In *The Courage to Teach*, Parker J. Palmer (2007) writes:

> Face to face with my students, my only resource at my immediate command: my identity, my selfhood. My ability to connect with my students . . . depends less on the methods I use than on the degree to which I know and trust my selfhood—am I willing to make it available and vulnerable in the service of learning?

As you try on and adapt the brain-changing words within these pages, modeling how to navigate elements of your own humanity, you'll inspire your students to follow suit.

## PART 1

# Establish and Maintain a Connected Classroom Community

Dozens of teachers have said a version of this to me: "I really care about classroom community, but I'm under so much pressure to cover curriculum that it's hard to find time to invest in it." I've felt this pressure, too. But the maddeningly simple truth—a truth that sometimes evades policymakers and administrators who operate far from the realities of the classroom—is that how children *feel* at school is inextricably linked to how they *do* at school. The notion that social, emotional, and academic learning can ever be separated from one another is a fallacy. "Social and emotional" work doesn't stand in opposition to "academic" learning; it's a prerequisite for academic success. Learning is inherently emotional (Immordino-Yang, 2015), and children who feel uniquely known and valued at school are able to take risks that lead to the most meaningful learning.

Students who feel comfortable and valued at school are able to take social and academic risks.

Neuroscientific research bears this out. The part of the brain we humans are so proud of—our frontal cortex, where our higher-level reasoning and learning take place—alights with neural activity when we feel secure and regulated. When children feel unwelcome, anxious, or shamed, the more primitive parts of the brain (including the amygdala, sometimes referred to as our "reptilian brain") can become the center of neural activity, pumping "fight or flight" hormones throughout their bodies. The more dysregulated or stressed any of us are, the more our prefrontal cortex functioning deteriorates (Arnsten, 2015).

Imagine a child whose identity, strengths, and interests aren't validated at school; who feels panicked about who to sit with during lunch time; who knows a public mistake means snickering peers. Is this student's hand zooming up to attempt to answer a tricky question? Is this child unselfconsciously sharing ideas in the context of a group project or taking risks in their creative writing? Certainly not. This student's energy is focused on a more fundamental, critical question: *How can I not feel isolated or humiliated today?*

> **Establishing and maintaining a connected classroom community is a foundational component of meaningful learning.**

Establishing and maintaining a connected classroom community is a foundational component of meaningful learning. Connectedness—the energy between people when they feel seen, heard, and valued (Brown, 2021)—is what lifts students out of feeling threatened or anxious and into a place where they are ready to learn. "Being connected is the most efficient and effective way to get information up to the cortex" (Perry & Winfrey, 2021). This section is all about language that opens the door to connection, which in turn opens the door to every other good thing that happens at school: joy, engagement, inspiration, you name it.

A connected classroom community boosts students' sense of belonging and capacity for risk-taking.

20      The Words That Shape Us

 **BRAIN-CHANGING WORDS**

*"Everything you bring to our classroom community matters. What is something you'd like us to know about you?"*

*"Something I'd like you to know about me is ___."*

---

For many students, it is revelatory to discover that "everything they bring to the classroom community"—their unique identities, strengths, interests, hopes, worries, and quirks—will inform their teacher's planning and influence how the school year unfolds. The phrase "something I'd like you to know about me" can inspire students to open up and connect deeply with peers and teachers. The repetition of this language, and the holding of space for all that students choose to share, helps children embrace their inherent self-worth: *They bring value to the classroom simply by being themselves.* They aren't empty vases for the teacher to fill up with skills; they already brim with important knowledge and contributions of their own. And ironically, decreasing pressure around achievement and increasing opportunities for students to feel uniquely known boost their capacity for risk-taking and resilience, essential ingredients of academic success.

While these words might seem especially bolstering to students who struggle at school, they're equally valuable for "high achievers"—students who are early readers and writers, whose hands fly up with correct answers, who have been complimented for their academic strengths for as long as they can remember. Surprisingly, these children can have the shakiest sense of self-esteem. This is because they've been showered with praise for *what they do*, not for *who they are*. These kids are excellent at following directions, but they can have trouble diving into open-ended, creative assignments that lack an obviously correct answer. And when their school careers are behind them, when there are no more directions from on high to follow, these über-achievers often struggle to determine what's interesting or meaningful to them professionally. After all, they've had plenty of time to exercise the muscle of compliance, but the muscle of curious introspection—of investigating their own interests and wonderings, and of assigning value to these parts of themselves—has atrophied.

As teachers, we need to celebrate these school superstars for being precisely themselves just as much as we need to celebrate their classmates who don't meet achievement metrics in the same glittering way. *All* students benefit from opportunities to explore their multifaceted identities and to share about the wonderful, idiosyncratic things that make them "them" and enrich the classroom community.

# Introducing This Language

While it's ideal to share this language with children at the beginning of the year, you can introduce it anytime. I remember telling students in April that, even though we'd been getting to know each other for months, there is always so much more to learn. As educator and writer Erika Christakis (2016) reminds us, "children are constantly changing and endlessly surprising," especially when we make space for them to reveal themselves to us and when we let go of the sometimes-rigid stories we tell about them.

You'll note that, when introducing this language, I make a point of modeling that contributions do not need to be academic or "big." As Valerie Worth's and William Carlos Williams's gorgeous "small" poems about safety pins, wheelbarrows, and plums teach us, when we're specific enough, we find the extraordinary in the ordinary. This holds true as children shape language around aspects of their identities.

Try a version of this:

**MS. LILY:** It's true that other children have gathered in this classroom before. They've sat on this very rug before. But the thinking and learning that we're jumping into together is brand-new. It's never happened before, ever, not in the history of the world! Because you have never been in this classroom before. Your particular interests, quirks, ideas, concerns, and wonderings have space to soar here and are already mixing together in wonderful, unexpected ways. I'm excited to teach *you*, not the curriculum, and everything you bring to this classroom community matters.

> **Something I'd like you to know about me is ___.**
>
> Ideas to consider:
>
> * What do you love to do?
> * What don't you love to do?
> * What is a hope you have?
> * Where are you "from"—a place, a memory, a tradition?
> * What is something that really makes you laugh?
> * What is an object that's important to you?
> * What do you wish others knew about you?
> * What is a small, secret talent of yours?
> * Anything else that springs to mind?
>
> \* Teachers of younger children might consider listing fewer ideas (choose a few that resonate) and sketching visual cues next to each idea.

Here's a phrase that can help us celebrate all the unique things we bring along to school each day: "Something I'd like you to know about me is ___." Think about something you'd like to share. Here are some ideas to consider (see anchor chart, left), though of course you can answer however you'd like. Listen to yourself: What springs to mind?

I'll begin. Something I'd like you to know about me is that I can sing very high in a squeaky tone, like a chipmunk. I'm proud of that silly talent! Who would like to volunteer their own "something I'd like you to know about me" statement?

**NOAH:** Something I'd like you to know about me is I'm not afraid of snakes, even though they're the number-two fear in the world. They smell with their tongues, and I think they're cool and beautiful, too.

**LUNA:** Something I'd like you to know about me is I love veggie straws. I wish we had veggie straws for snack every day. Also, I speak two languages.

**THEODORE:** Something I'd like you to know about me is that I get annoyed when everyone makes a big deal about my baby brother and I'm just standing there, sort of invisible.

## Kids' Turn

Here are some ways children can use and internalize this language.

- In the context of a morning-meeting greeting:

  **JONESE:** Good morning, Anaiya! Something I'd like you to know about me is that I know how to clean my pet rat's cage all by myself.

- In the context of a morning-meeting, after-lunch, or closing-circle "share," create a schedule so children know when their turn is coming up. Invite each student to share three "something I'd like you to know about me" statements and encourage peers to offer supportive feedback. (Consider using window/mirror language, page 39, and/or "I love how/I felt/I never knew" language, page 47.)

- In the context of preparing to work together as a group, each child can share a "something I'd like you to know about me" statement:

  **ETHAN:** Something I'd like you to know about me is that moving helps me focus, so during our book club I'm going to fiddle with this rubber band I got in OT. But I'm still listening.

## Curricular Connections

Apply the language across subject areas with these ideas.

### Poetry Invitation: Things to Know About Me/Us

Poetry, with its endless possibilities and economy of language, can feel like a breath of fresh air for students. In particular, the straightforward structure of a list poem gets pencils up and moving. A teacher recently told me that when she asked her fourth graders to write a paragraph about themselves, more than half of the class struggled to get started. When she asked the kids to jot down a quick list poem, "Five Things to Know About Me" (no full sentences needed; kids could jot down whichever five things first popped into their minds), nearly every student jumped right in.

There are many ways to invite children to write "Things to Know About Me/Us" list poetry. Young children can visually represent their thinking or verbally share a statement as you record their contributions on an anchor chart and create a collaborative poem. Older children can write their own list poems in their writer's notebooks, and then choose one line to contribute to a class-wide poem. Children of all ages can create self-portrait list poems by gluing their statements around images of themselves or of things they love.

Examples of "Things to Know About Me/Us" list poems

**Things to Know About Us**
One Line Per 306-er

Sometimes I just need to read my book
You should know I'm working on using less electronics
I'm happiest when I am **not** with my brother (I'm kind of kidding)
I have synesthesia
Sometimes I play pranks
I am an artist, a singer, maybe an athlete
I am from Turkey
I love my mom
Sometimes I write in my fort
You should know I'm a triplet. I have a brother and a sister
I am happiest when I'm in my own world
I worry about homework

The Words That Shape Us

**Student-as-Teacher Initiative: "Something I bring to this classroom community is ___."**

Elementary schoolers brim with so much knowledge and expertise that the traditional curriculum does not touch upon. One way to celebrate all that your students already know—to clearly send the message "everything you bring to our classroom community matters"—is to initiate a Student-as-Teacher routine. Once a week (or once every other week), invite a child to teach the class about any topic that resonates with them. Topics from former students include synesthesia, Michael Jackson's moonwalking moves, and Toadette (from *Mario Kart*). This is not a research project or connected to curricula in any way; children are simply sharing knowledge they already possess. During choice time and quiet time, my co-teacher Anneliese and I would offer that week's presenter the option of creating a poster or a slide deck. Some students chose to use neither tool, and instead dreamed up their own way to present the information to their classmates. Children had complete autonomy, which is one reason why this initiative felt so exciting.

In June, Anneliese and I asked our students to complete a survey about the year. We asked: *What projects or curricula did you especially enjoy (or not)? What suggestions do you have for us?* Nearly every child referenced the Student-as-Teacher initiative as a "favorite thing." For our kids, it was a thrill to experience a new way of "success" at school: *Wait, I'm in control here? I can succeed in a way that feels personal and meaningful to me, as opposed to succeeding by simply following your directions?* Perhaps most importantly, the presentations allowed kids to see one another more clearly, to better understand their peers' unique perspectives, interests, and strengths.

(left) Tirzah teaches the class about old-fashioned clothes.
(right) Zora teaches about the importance of positive representation in literature and media.

PART 1: Establish and Maintain a Connected Classroom Community

## Partnering With Families

Share these strategies with families for weaving the language into their home lives.

**Family members can share "something I'd like you to know about me" statements with one another.**

In his book *Far From the Tree*, Andrew Solomon points out that *reproduction* is a misleading term for bringing a child into the world, for the word implies that it is "ourselves we would like to see live forever, not someone with a personality of his own." There is no such thing as reproduction, only *production*. Children are mysterious creatures who are profoundly separate from their parents. This separateness can be difficult to face: An athletic parent may have a child who refuses to join a sports team; a neurotypical parent may have a neuroatypical child. Even within parent-child relationships full of shared interests and strengths ("she gets her love of math from me"; "we've got the same extroverted spirit"), there is no real overlap, no blurring of personhood. The parent ends, the child begins, and there is always space in between. "Something I'd like you to know about me" language can inject understanding, humor, and heart into that space.

**JADE:** Something I'd like you to know about me is that even though I'm the oldest, I'd still like my own "wake-up-cozy-singing-time" like Annabelle gets. With a blanket on the sofa, please.

**PARENT:** Something I'd like you to know about me is that if I ever seem sad, it's never because of anything you did, and it's not your job to fix it. Sadness comes and goes, and I love you always.

**LILIANA:** Something I'd like you to know about me is that when you always ask me to play the piano when your friends come over, I feel like that's the thing you think is coolest about me.

Inevitably, children may use this language to share something surprising with their parents; something that makes the space between them feel more like an ocean than a river. In her beautiful book *The Anti-Romantic Child: A Memoir of Unexpected Joy*, Priscilla Gilman shares that the German poet Rainer Maria Rilke's words (from *Letters*) helped her embrace the distance between her and her son Benj, who has hyperlexia, a rare developmental disorder. Some parents may find this excerpt comforting, too:

> Once the realization is accepted that even between the closest human beings infinite distances continue to exist, a wonderful living side by side can grow up, if they succeed in loving the distance between them, which makes it possible for each to see the other whole against the sky.

Gilman writes: "The distance, space, gap between me and my child is no longer a terrifying void, an unbridgeable gulf, a yawning emptiness, but rather a capacious and blessed opening, an aperture of respect and marvel." Gilman's memoir helps me hold onto the truth that I can see my children clearly only if I take a step *back* from them, if I remember that they are their own wondrous, singular people, not extensions of myself.

And outside of parenthood, Rilke's and Gilman's words can serve as guides for anyone who is interested in "loving the distance" between themselves and others—be they students, colleagues, friends, partners, or family.

**Families can use "everything you bring to this family matters" language.**

This language is particularly helpful in the context of children comparing themselves to a sibling or opening up about what's on their mind. For instance, when a child is visibly upset and unwilling to share why, a parent might say:

**PARENT:** Remember, everything you bring to this family matters. Every feeling is welcome here. When you're ready, I'm here to listen.

Parents can even create their own "What We Bring to This Family" shared list poem (one line per family member). Lovingly wrapping words around the idiosyncratic, you-being-precisely-you aspects of their kids' identities (instead of the shiny, achievement-oriented parts) helps kids feel a deep sense of "enough-ness" and belonging. They carry this sense of familial belonging within them like a hidden magic power; an antidote to people-pleasing and to inauthentically twisting themselves into something else to belong socially at school.

> **Things we bring to this family:**
> *A love of cooler ranch Doritos*
>
> *Surprising everyone when I disappear behind the curtains*
>
> *The strangest (greatest?) improvised Robin Hood stories*
>
> *Endless kisses for freckly cheeks*

One family's shared list poem

**PARENT:** You bring so many wonderful things to this family just by being yourself. In your own words, what is one little thing that only you bring?

**Children can listen closely for family-specific, celebratory language.**

What are some phrases or sayings within their family vernacular that help them name and clearly communicate what makes them—as individuals or as a family unit—unique? Children can bring this language back into the classroom.

 **BRAIN-CHANGING WORDS**

# "We all have outer shells and inner swirls."
# "Just because ___ doesn't mean ___."

Even very young children are aware of the stories others tell about them:

> "He's the smartest."
> "She can never sit still."
> "He's so unmotivated—if only he would get his head off his desk and *try*."

Children also know that their exterior, representative selves (their "outer shells") reveal only a fraction of who they really are, and many students long for language to name the tension between their outer shells and their inner lives (their "inner swirls"). And as children look beyond themselves and to one another, outer shells/inner swirls language gives them words to shape around the idea that there is always so much more behind a classmate's outward behavior or demeanor: Inner swirls are invisible yet chock-full of complexity and surprise.

As children become comfortable naming and sharing about their outer shells and inner swirls, "just because" language helps them clearly and kindly correct misconceptions and share what's true. As my student Sama told his classmates: "Just because I'm quiet on the rug doesn't mean I don't have ideas in my head." And I stopped in my tracks when I read what my student Aaron, a big-hearted child who struggled to self-regulate and who had been described by a specialist as having "serious behavior issues"—wrote in his writer's notebook: "Just because I get upset doesn't mean I'm mean."

> **We compare our inner swirls to someone else's outer shell, though we often have no idea what's swirling within that person.**

This language not only helps children express themselves and see others in more nuanced ways, it also helps them navigate the quicksand of comparison. Comparison is painful because it tricks us into a false equivalency: We compare our inner swirls to someone else's outer shell, though we often have no idea what's swirling within that person. The precise, delineating nature of outer shell/inner swirls language helps children understand the faultiness of most comparisons, and just-because language reminds them of all they *don't* know about someone else's inner life. As my student Alexis wisely explained: "You can't compare your insides to other people's just outsides. Just because everyone looks calm doesn't mean they are."

If social media has taught us anything, it's that the most frequent, sunny projections of our outsides can actually have an inverse correlation with well-being. Forty percent of children ages 8–12 already use social media, which, according to Surgeon General Vivek Murthy (2023), poses a "profound risk of harm to the mental health and well-being of children." Often, it's what we assume alienates us from others (inner swirls like

The Words That Shape Us

ambivalence or insecurity) that actually connects us most deeply; those uncomfortable feelings are natural, healthy parts of being alive. But when young people consume social media, this complexity is missing, and children can feel isolated by the (mistaken) impression that their inner swirls are theirs and theirs alone.

One small, powerful countermeasure to this isolation is language that helps children have open, connected conversations with one another. These conversations inevitably lead to the epiphany that a feeling or an experience a child thought was uniquely hers is actually shared with peers. Good books can also prompt this recognition—in an interview with *Life* magazine, James Baldwin (Howard, 1963) put it this way:

> You think your pain and your heartbreak are unprecedented in the history of the world, but then you read. It was Dostoevsky and Dickens who taught me that the things that tormented me most were the very things that connected me with all the people who were alive, who had ever been alive.

Outer shell/inner swirls language and just-because language help children find the connectedness Baldwin speaks of—with one another and within the books they're reading. Students can easily and intuitively use this language to explore the complexities of characters: "Just because Beezus tells Ramona she ruined her life doesn't mean she actually means it; her inner swirls are just all mad and frustrated in that moment." And of course, seeking to understand the nuance behind make-believe behavior makes it easier to see nuance in real-life behavior: "Just because my big sister wants to be alone with her friends sometimes doesn't mean she doesn't love me so much."

## Introducing This Language

You can introduce "outer shell/inner swirls" and "just-because" phrases separately or simultaneously. Some teachers prefer to share outer shell/inner swirls language in the context of analyzing a character in a read-aloud, and then children can try on the language themselves. Other teachers like to complete their own Outer Shell/Inner Swirls Identity Map (see page 130 for the reproducible template)—a great way to appropriately and honestly normalize vulnerability—and then, after gathering students' observations, use just-because language to describe their map. (I've modeled this approach on the following page.) When children create their own Outer Shell/Inner Swirls Identity Maps and share them with one another, they discover all sorts of new connections and understandings. These maps brim with great ideas for writing, to boot.

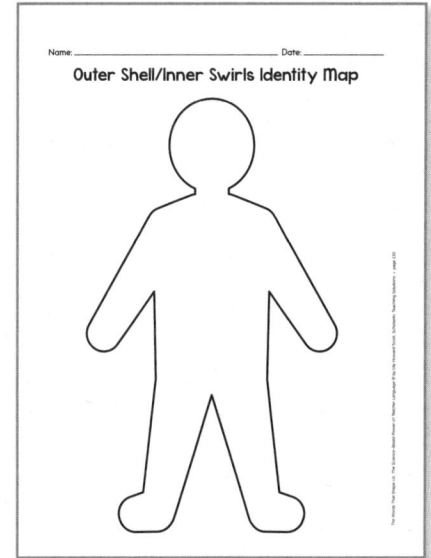

See page 130 for this reproducible template.

PART 1: Establish and Maintain a Connected Classroom Community

Try a version of this:

**MS. LILY:** Today, I'm going to introduce some language that will help us understand ourselves *and* one another better. We all walk around with "outer shells"—the parts of us that are easy to see: what we look like, what we wear, how we talk, our demeanor, aspects of our identity that we tend to share with people right away. And behind those outer shells, we have "inner swirls"—the parts of us that are not easy to see: our wonderings, longings, cherished memories, important experiences, and so much more. Watch how, inspired by the ideas to consider on this anchor chart (see below), I complete my own Outer Shell/Inner Swirls Identity Map. [Using a document camera, project a copy of the template on page 130 on the board and start filling it in.]

You'll see how, on my outer shell, I'm writing that I'm a teacher. I tend to tell people that fact about myself pretty quickly. And in my inner swirls, I'm writing that I sometimes feel nervous speaking in front of a crowd. Occasionally, people can make assumptions (in other words, tell a story that isn't necessarily accurate) based on an element of our outer shell. But we owe it to ourselves—and to others—to move through the world in a kind, direct way. Here's a simple thing you can say to address assumptions head on and reveal what's true: *Just because ___ doesn't mean ___.* For instance: *Just because I'm a teacher doesn't mean I don't get nervous about speaking in front of a crowd sometimes.*

**Ideas to consider when creating your Outer Shell/Inner Swirls Identity Map:**

**Outer Shell** (the parts of us that are easy to see)

* What you look like
* What you like to wear
* Some aspects of your identity you tend to reveal quickly (perhaps age, grade level, number of people in your family, major interests, and so on)

**Inner Swirls** (the parts of us that are not so easy to see)

* Feelings
* Wonderings
* Hopes
* Pet peeves
* Cherished memories
* People, places, things, and traditions that are important to you

A young child colored his identity map to reflect himself and then drew elements of his inner swirls on round stickers, which he glued inside the figure.

MS. LILY: Take a look at my former student Quinn's map. What do you notice?

EZRA: On his outer shell he wrote that he loves Harry Potter, so maybe he talks about Harry Potter a lot?

ALLISON: In his inner swirls he says he's usually very good and not naughty, so it's a bigger deal when he does things like sneak candy into bed. I really relate because I feel like it's a bigger deal when I do stuff like that than when my little sister does.

MS. LILY: Yes! On his outer shell, Quinn writes that he can be shy, kind, and nice, and that he's often asked by teachers to share his schoolwork. In his inner swirls, he writes that he loves to dance and that he can sometimes get in trouble for being a bit naughty at home. Here's what I learned: *Just because Quinn can be shy doesn't mean he doesn't love to dance.* Also: *Just because he's kind and nice doesn't mean he can't also be a touch mischievous!*

Today, you'll have the option of creating your own Outer Shell/Inner Swirls Identity Maps. If it's helpful, you can draw or write in response to the ideas to consider on the anchor chart (see page 30), or you can create straight from your heart. As always: It's up to you.

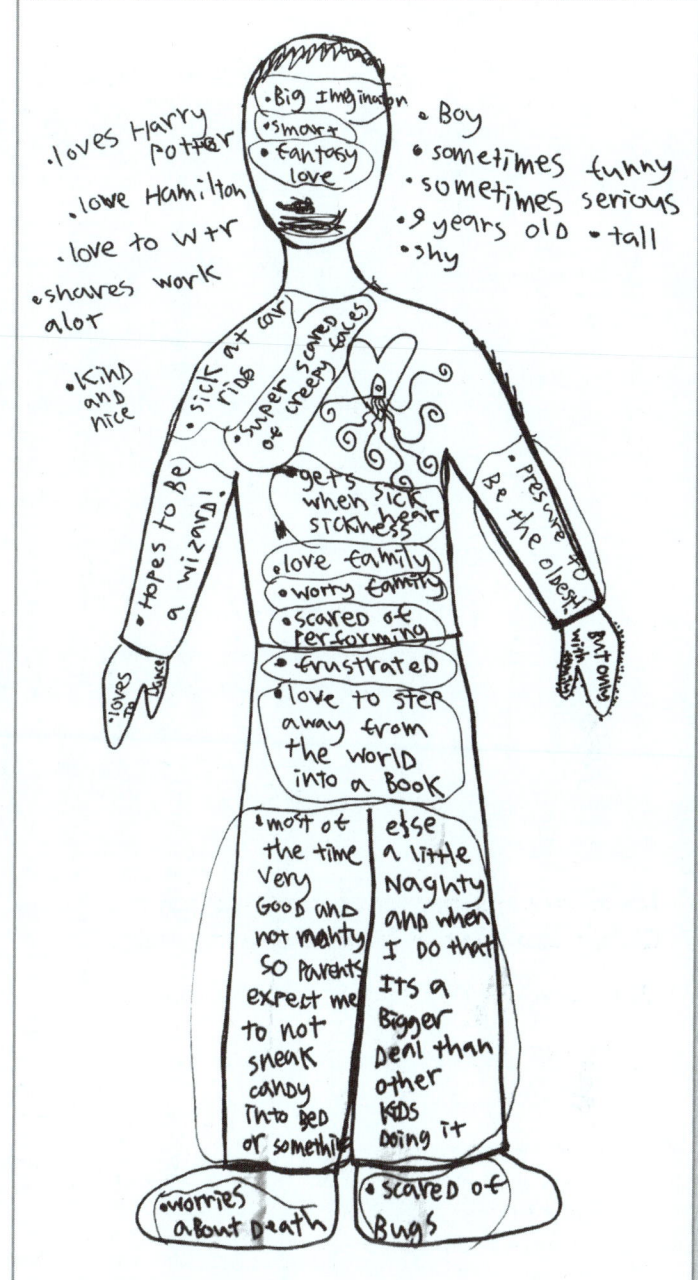

Quinn's Outer Shell/Inner Swirls Identity Map

PART 1: Establish and Maintain a Connected Classroom Community

# Kids' Turn

Here are some ways children can use and internalize this language.

- Children can share their Outer Shell/Inner Swirls Identity Maps with one another in small groups, as a gallery walk, or one at a time under a document camera. Afterwards, invite peers to offer supportive, specific feedback. (Consider using window/mirror language, page 39, and/or "I love how/I felt/I never knew" language, page 47.)

- In partnerships, kids can share "just because" statements inspired by their maps:

    AALIYAH: Just because my outer shell looks cheerful and like I don't mind something, actually in my inner swirls, my feelings might be a little hurt.

- In the context of resolving conflict:

    LUCAS: Just because I interrupted you doesn't mean I don't think your ideas are good. I guess I was especially excited to share mine. I'm sorry!

    ABIGAIL: I had a lot of frustrated thoughts and feelings bouncing around my inner swirls at recess. I needed some alone time. But I wasn't mad at you.

- As self-talk:

    CORA: Just because I'm having trouble decoding right now doesn't mean I'm not a great reader-thinker.

Depending on what your students are grappling with, you can elicit children's suggestions to create self-talk prompts to display in the classroom (see anchor chart below). The secret power of a self-talk anchor chart is that kids can't help but reread it all the time, often in regulated, successful moments. In harder moments, the language from the chart is already within them, ready to be called upon.

---

**Things to say to yourself when schoolwork feels *challenging* or *confusing*:**

* Just because I'm making a lot of mistakes doesn't mean I'm not learning. Mistakes help me learn, actually.

* Just because my brain sometimes tells me I'm not a math person <u>doesn't mean it's true</u>.

* Just because I don't have a perfect plan for what I'm going to write doesn't mean that I can't get started anyway. Ideas will come to me as I go.

You might also collaborate with an individual student to create a specific, miniature anchor chart (like the one below that the child can tape somewhere private (perhaps inside a desk or folder). In moments of dysregulation, the student can reference this personalized resource.

> Just because I *feel* anger doesn't mean I *am* my anger. I can always make a calm choice.
>
> 1. Go to the calm-down corner.
> 2. Squeeze my squeezie to the rhythm of decade counting to 100 (10, 20, 30, . . .).
> 3. Ask for help.
>
> **Just because something goes wrong does not mean it is a crisis.** Point to the problem size below and consider what you'd like to do! **You've got this.**
>
>
> **PEBBLE PROBLEM** (Ex: losing a pencil)
> * List possible independent solutions
> * You can solve this on your own!
> * NOT an emergency
>
>
> **ROCK PROBLEM** (Ex: your turn is skipped)
> * Raise your hand for help
> * Collaborate with teacher or classmate
> * NOT an emergency
>
> **MOUNTAIN PROBLEM**
> (Ex: someone is seriously hurt)
> * Immediately walk to a teacher to share
> * OK to interrupt!

Child-specific, mini self-talk anchor chart, taped within desk (or wherever the child would like it to be)

PART 1: Establish and Maintain a Connected Classroom Community

# Curricular Connections

Apply the language across subject areas with these ideas.

### Character Map: Outer Shell/Inner Swirls

In conversations about literature, outer shell/inner swirls language helps children explore the distinction between a character's external representation and inner life. A prekindergartner recently told me, "Gaston thinks he loves Belle, but he doesn't. He loves her outer shell because she's beautiful, but he doesn't love her insides at all."

Younger children can create Outer Shell/Inner Swirls Character Maps (see page 131 for the reproducible template) by drawing inside and outside the figure or by narrating ideas to a teacher in the context of a shared-writing exercise. Older students can complete maps about characters in their independent reading book, and also use this template as they dream up characters for their own fiction writing.

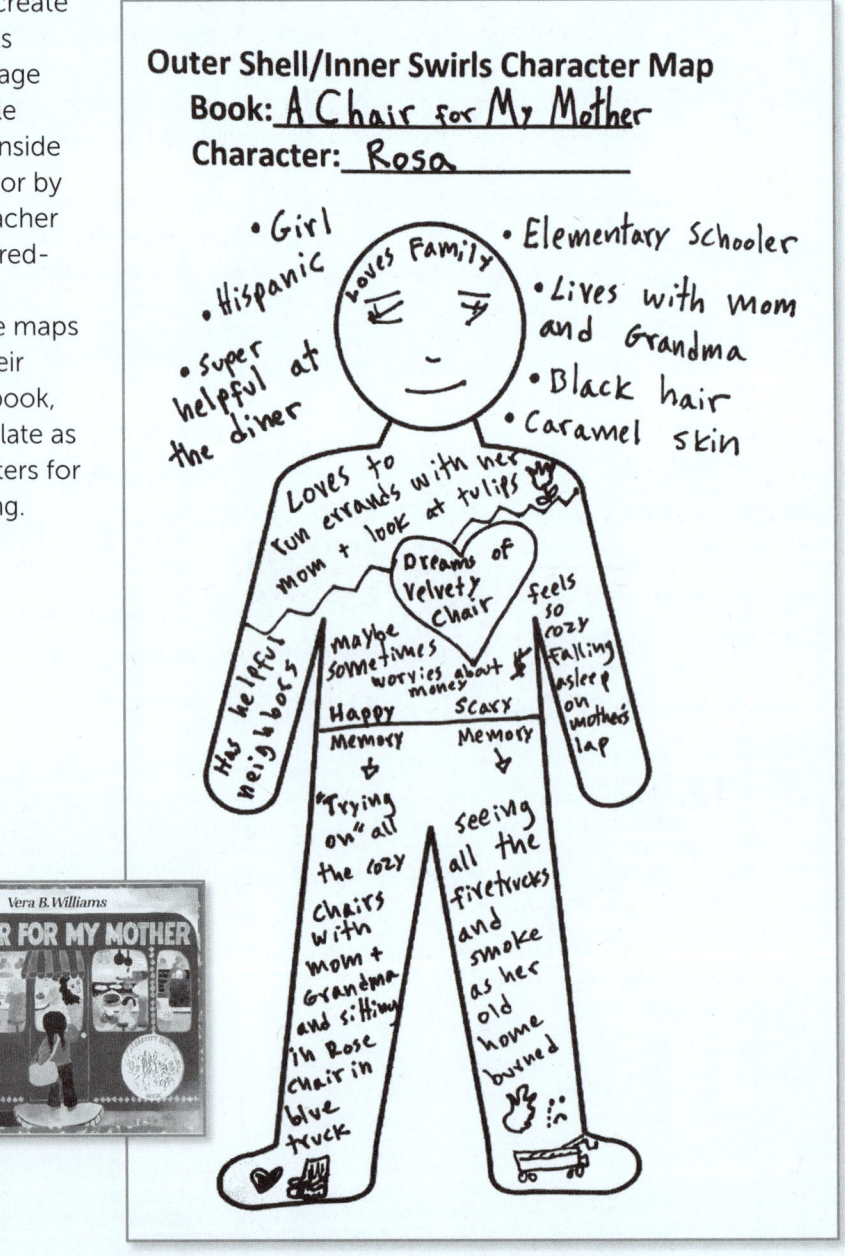

An Outer Shell/Inner Swirls Character Map of Rosa from *A Chair for My Mother*

### Reading Response: Noticing and Interrupting Assumptions

Younger children can use just-because language to verbally notice and interrupt assumptions about characters in read-alouds; older students can use the Reading Response: Interrupting Assumptions template (page 132).

**Noticing & Interrupting Our Assumptions About Characters**

Notice: What assumptions are you making about characters?
- What evidence in the text supports these conclusions?

Notice: What new information disrupts some of these assumptions?
- What wonderings and theories come to mind as you process this information?

Tying Things Together: What deeper understandings do you arrive at?
- How can these understandings inform the stories we tell about people we encounter in our own lives?

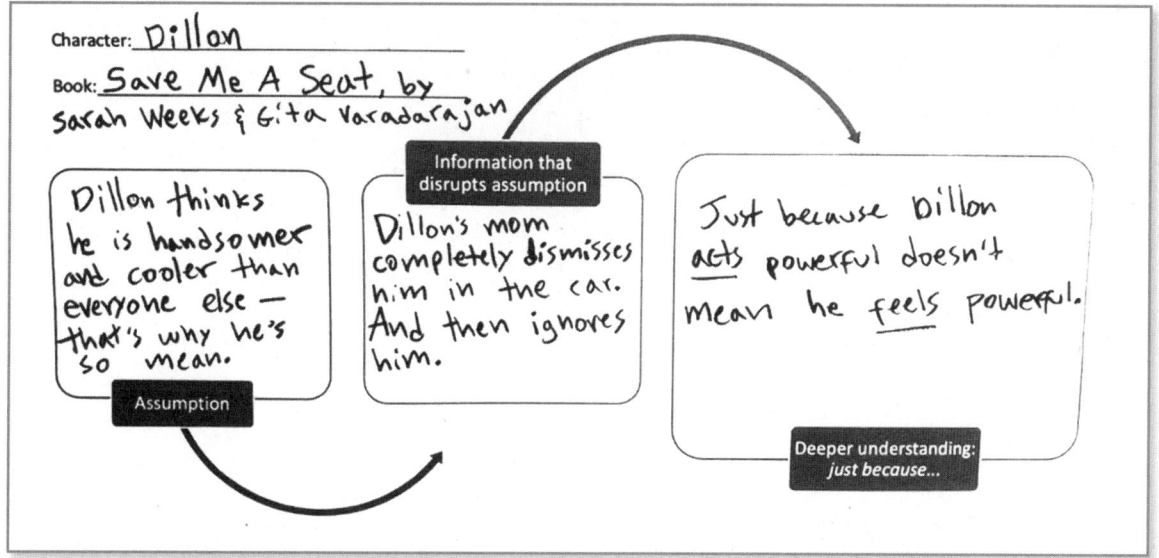

Just-because language helps young readers interrupt assumptions about characters.

PART 1: Establish and Maintain a Connected Classroom Community

**Poetry Invitation: Just Because**

Students can write introspective poetry by jotting down a few just-because statements. The poems below by my former third-grade students capture and memorialize the important ideas they wished to communicate about themselves.

**Just Because**
By Aaron

Just because I'm Puerto Rican
Doesn't mean I speak Spanish

Just because I get upset
Doesn't mean I'm mean

Just because I'm not good at sports
Doesn't mean I'm not good at anything

Just because I take care of my little sister
Doesn't mean I take care of everything.

**Did you know?**
By Sama

Did you know I'm a musician?

Just because I don't talk on the rug
Doesn't mean I don't have ideas in my head

Just because I live far away
Doesn't mean I can't go to this school
(I am just late)

Just because I am half-Russian
Doesn't mean I don't speak good English

Just because I am not really good at math
Doesn't mean I'm not
Very very good
At other things.

**Me and My Dad**
By Zora

Just because my dad
Has a different skin color than me
Does not mean
He
Is
Not
My
Dad.

Notice that my student Dashiell's poem (right) does not include "just because" language. He dreamed up other words to express the idea that wonderful things lie just beneath, or accompany, some of his challenges. Yes, he sketches a lot in class so he can focus—and all that practice means that maybe he'll be an illustrator one day. Yes, writing can be hard for him, but he still has good ideas. Yes, his brain sometimes tells him to do the wrong thing, but he's still nice. Just as Harper conjured up her own "President Decider" language, Dashiell takes the essence of a just-because poem and breathes new life into it.

> **I am me**
> By Dashiell
>
> I like reading
> I also like art
> Sometimes I have to draw so I can focus in class.
> This gives me a lot of time to practice drawing.
> Maybe I will be an illustrator when I grow up.
>
> My brain is so full of ideas it might explode.
> Writing things down can be hard.
> But that doesn't mean I don't have good ideas.
>
> You should know
> Sometimes my brain tells me to do the wrong thing.
> But that doesn't mean
> I'm never nice.
>
> I am not perfect
> But I am me.

In some schools, embracing students' adaptations and letting them stray from a particular format can pose challenges around grading. But requiring standardization inhibits students' creativity and teaches them not to listen to their own instincts. It's an incredibly powerful experience for a child to suggest an adaptation and have their idea not only tolerated but *welcomed*, even if doing so makes assessment criteria a bit more vague. (Though I'd argue, how can one possibly grade a just-because identity poem, anyway? In *The Tyranny of Metrics*, Jerry Z. Muller points out: "Not everything that is important is measurable, and much that is measurable is unimportant.")

## Partnering With Families

Share these strategies with families for weaving the language into their home lives.

**Children can bring home blank Outer Shell/Inner Swirls Identity Map templates to share with parents or siblings.**

The best way to learn something is to teach it. When children teach their parents or siblings how to complete an Outer Shell/Inner Swirls Identity Map (page 130), sharing examples of their inner swirls and explaining that everyone has them, those children internalize the idea that all people—yes, even their parents!—have rich inner lives. And as parents appropriately yet vulnerably create maps, children may be surprised to notice that some of their parents' inner swirls resonate with them. This "I see part of myself in you!" moment boosts connectedness.

**Families can reference outer shell/inner swirls language in moments of repair.**

PARENT: I'm really sorry I yelled. You couldn't see this just by looking at my outer shell, but I've had an especially hard day and was feeling frustrated about a problem at work. I should have explained this to you instead of losing my temper out of nowhere. You did nothing wrong, and I love you.

**Family members can share just-because statements with one another.**

I once heard comedian and writer David Sedaris observe that family roles outlive their usefulness. The closeness of a nuclear unit means that it can be difficult for family members to let one another grow and change. In larger families, children tend to "fill the available space" and lean into the lanes that siblings haven't already occupied (Dunn, 1983). If an older sister is dubbed "the brainy one," a younger sister might think, *Well, that's taken*, and lean into another role—the creative one, perhaps, or the difficult one. The irony of tracking kids into lanes is that children are shape-shifters whose interests and strengths change constantly. Yet under the "I am as I hear you talk about me" umbrella, they play the roles adults assign to them. Just-because language can inspire both children and parents to communicate a broader breadth of possibility.

PARENT: I love your big heart. But just because you're such a wonderful helper with your little brother doesn't mean you always have to be the helper. When you'd like to play independently, you can always kindly tell Henry that you'd like a break from pretending with him.

GAEL: Just because I'm really good at soccer doesn't mean it's something I love to do.

To Colorado Poet Laureate Andrea Gibson, caring for someone isn't so much about understanding them inside and out but about letting the person always be new to us. Gibson (2019) writes: "There is so much love in consistently asking 'who are you now?' . . . to love someone isn't so much to know them, as it is to know their never-ending becoming." A student who exhibited extremely challenging behavior in the fall may surprise their teacher with their self-regulation in the spring. A child who has been dubbed by parents as the family's "ray of sunshine" (in contrast to a sensitive, often-screaming sibling) may feel obligated to always present cheerfulness; to not share about the hard things they're grappling with—after all, that's their sibling's lane. When we stop essentializing one another and instead make space for "never-ending becoming," we make space for growth.

### BRAIN-CHANGING WORDS

## "What are the windows and mirrors within our classroom community?"

In Emily Style's 1988 essay "Curriculum as Window and Mirror," she explains that to feel validated and welcome at school, all students need "mirrors"—reflections of their identities and experiences. But to cultivate an appreciation of varied perspectives and lived realities, they also need "windows"—insights into identities and experiences that are not their own. This "window/mirror" metaphor (which Rudine Sims Bishop elaborated upon in her groundbreaking essay "Windows, Mirrors, and Sliding Glass Doors") is a gold mine. The language can be used across every subject area to celebrate both connections and illuminations in a beautifully inclusive, nuanced way.

When I was a classroom teacher, I typically began each school year by talking about the importance of seeing ourselves mirrored in the books we read (Bishop, 1990) and by asking children to bring in from home or find in the classroom a "mirror book" that reflected something important about them. It was completely up to the kids to decide on the mirror. Sometimes children chose books that reflected their family structures or ethnicities; sometimes they chose books about a beloved hobby. When curating our classroom library, my co-teachers and I worked hard to ensure that every child felt positively represented. But a few years ago, while teaching in Washington, D.C., I failed at providing this representation.

My former student Leo, who is transgender (an aspect of identity he had chosen not to share about in our classroom, and one we'd been asked by an administrator not to bring up with him) wrote in his self-portrait list poem (below): "You should know that I am transgender." When I saw this line, I said, "Thank you for sharing this part of yourself with us. Would you like to tell me more?" Leo replied, "I'm transgender, and I don't have a mirror book in this class."

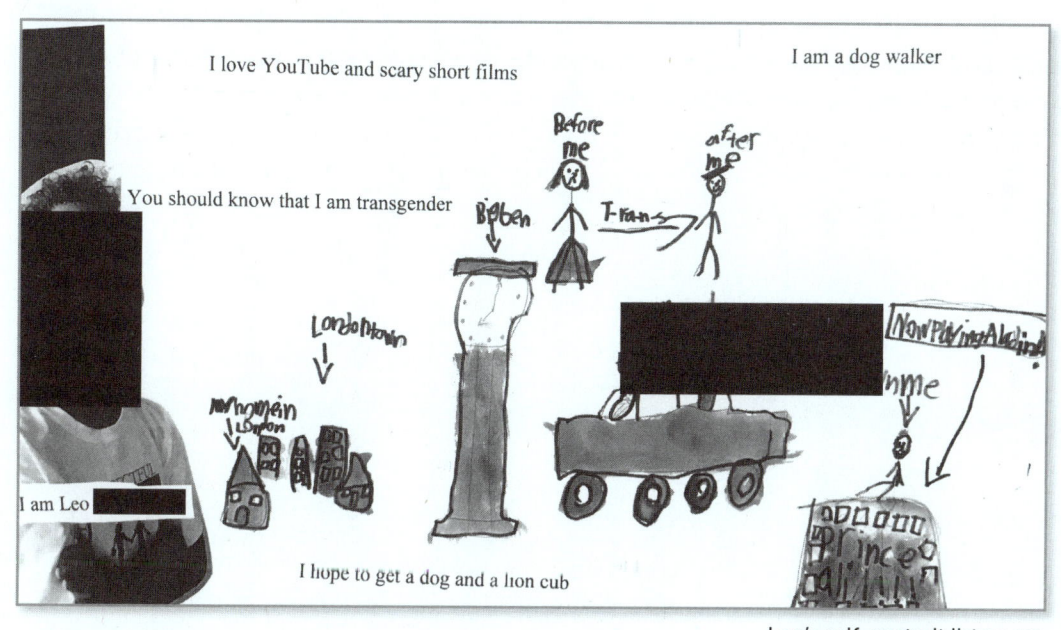

Leo's self-portrait list poem

PART 1: Establish and Maintain a Connected Classroom Community

I felt a wave of shame. I hadn't wanted to "out" Leo, make him feel pressured to share, or initiate a classroom discussion he wasn't ready to have. But by not providing a book that mirrored this particular part of his identity, I hadn't validated his full self at school. My co-teacher Casey and I set about correcting this. Leo told us about a mirror book he had at home: "I want to share *Jack (Not Jackie)* with the class, just like Cate shared her book about being adopted." Together, Leo, Casey, and I planned his "mirror book" share. We notified parents about the upcoming read-aloud and provided them resources to support follow-up conversations with their children at home. To prepare, Leo reread *Jack (Not Jackie)* and posted sticky notes on certain pages, jotting about his mirror connections: "This is a mirror because my mom also lets me shop in the part of the store that's right for me."

On the day of his share, Leo sat beside me as I read the picture book aloud, and I paused now and then so he could read his sticky-note mirror jots. Leo, a vivacious, outgoing child, was perfectly still and read his jots in a near-whisper. His typically bouncy, chatty classmates sat motionless on the rug, except for the occasional wiggle of fingers in his direction, our classroom signal for "I'm sending love your way." It was one of those rare moments in which every single child is united on a similar emotional plane, intently focused on the same thing. Leo's courage was palpable. Everyone seemed to sense what an enormous risk he was taking in that moment.

Casey and I avoided eye contact. We worried if we connected, the lumps in our throats might spill over into tears—so moved were we by Leo's bravery, so hopeful were we that his classmates would respond with kindness. After the read-aloud, Leo said, "I'm ready for questions and comments." Luke, a friendly, charismatic student, raised his hand and said, "I'm so honored that you shared that with us. And I think Leo is a great name for you because I know how much you love lions." Another child said, "I have a window to you because I'm not transgender. But I know what it's like when my mom lets me shop in the part of the store that's my favorite, so that's a little mirror." Other hands shot up. Leo's classmates affirmed his choice to share and revealed their own windows and mirrors to his experience.

I thought of something a colleague had told me years earlier: If you ask a child to walk to the classroom window and look out, they'll tell you what they see (a tree, a building, a car). But then if you ask the child to look closer, they'll see the faintest reflection of themselves. The students' dexterity with window/mirror language helped them understand that Leo's share was indeed mostly a window but also, from some angles, a slight mirror. *Everyone* in the room could relate to wanting to be listened to, wanting to be heard by grown-ups around them. Leo's body relaxed, and he beamed from ear to ear. After lunch, he returned to this note on his desk from Carson (left).

Leo moved throughout the rest of his day with a confidence and ease only possible in those who feel known and valued. Without window/mirror language, I don't know if he would have chosen to share about this aspect of his identity with his classmates. And even if he had, I am sure his classmates wouldn't have been able to respond to him in such a nuanced, deeply supportive way. Window/mirror language guided them away from "either/or" thinking (*You are like me, or you're not*) and toward "both/and" thinking (*We are different, and we are the same*).

Leo used window/mirror language in a "big" way. But there are so many little ways to weave this language throughout daily routines and curricula, empowering kids to honor both connection and difference. One May afternoon many years ago, after a particularly rambunctious recess (any teacher reading this knows the feverish, school-is-almost-out energy I'm talking about), I asked two students to join me in the hallway so I could help them resolve a dispute. One child explained how the other had pushed him, and the second student waited patiently for him to finish. Then the second student—who had fallen on the first child accidentally—said, "What you just described is a window for me. That's not what I remember happening." I was bowled over by his diplomacy in that moment. He could have easily said, "You're lying!" or "That's not true!" but his dexterity with window/mirror language helped navigate a challenging moment with more grace than many adults might have mustered.

> **Window/mirror language guided them away from "either/or" thinking (*You are like me, or you're not*) and toward "both/and" thinking (*We are different, and we are the same*).**

## Introducing This Language

I love introducing window/mirror language to kids of all ages with Amy Krouse Rosenthal's wonderful picture book *One of Those Days*. It's about how everyone has hard days: "annoying sibling day," "itchy sweater day," "sad for no reason day." Thankfully, as Krouse puts it, "every single one of those days eventually turns into night, and every single night turns into a brand-new day." As I read, I teach kids the silent hand signals for *mirror* (see below left) and *window* (below center). I've read this book aloud for over a decade now, and every listener has found both windows and mirrors within its pages.

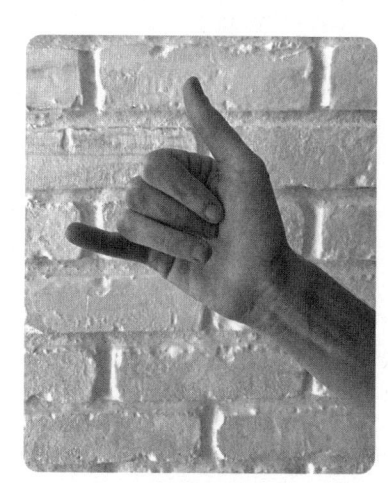

Our class's sign for *mirror* . . .

. . . and *window*

I use Rosenthal's picture book to introduce kids to window/mirror language.

PART 1: Establish and Maintain a Connected Classroom Community

Try a version of this:

**MS. LILY:** (holding a small mirror) What do you see when you look at this mirror? Your wonderful self. But mirrors aren't just these shiny objects we use when we're combing our hair. We can find "mirrors"—reflections of our identities and experiences—everywhere we look: in books, in movies, in other people, in *anything*. Now, I need a volunteer to look out of the window: What do you see?

**GRACE:** A tree and a baby in a stroller!

**MS. LILY:** Yes. We see something new, something that's not us. We can also find "windows"—or insights into new identities and experiences—everywhere we look. Mirrors are important because they help us feel understood, celebrated, and connected. Windows are important because they provide much-needed fresh air, new understandings about other perspectives and experiences.

As I read *One of Those Days*, be on the lookout for windows and mirrors, and be ready with *this* silent signal for a mirror and *this* silent signal for a window. If a page provides both a window and a mirror, wonderful! You can give both signals. We'll be weaving these signals into every part of the school day: morning meeting, writing, math, social studies, closing circle. You can even use these signals at home. After all, windows and mirrors are all around you, if you know to look for them.

## Kids' Turn

Here are some ways children can use and internalize this language.

- As children learn about each other at the beginning of the school year, they can share (verbally or through silent signals) the windows and mirrors they discover. For instance, after a prekindergartner shares a stuffed animal from home at morning meeting, the teacher might say:

    **MS. LILY:** Please raise a hand if you'd like to share a window or a mirror. Do you also have a stuffed animal you love at home? How is it similar or different?

    **LOGAN:** I have a mirror because I have a bunny, too. My bunny is black, not purple.

- In the context of a read-aloud, independent reading, or social studies lesson, children can share the mirrors and windows they find in characters and historical figures.

- In the context of discussing math strategies, kids can use window/mirror language to celebrate a variety of ways to solve problems.

    **EMERY:** Give me a mirror if you also solved with a number line. Give a window if you used another strategy!

- Children can respond to one another's schoolwork with window/mirror sticky-note jots that celebrate connections and illuminations:

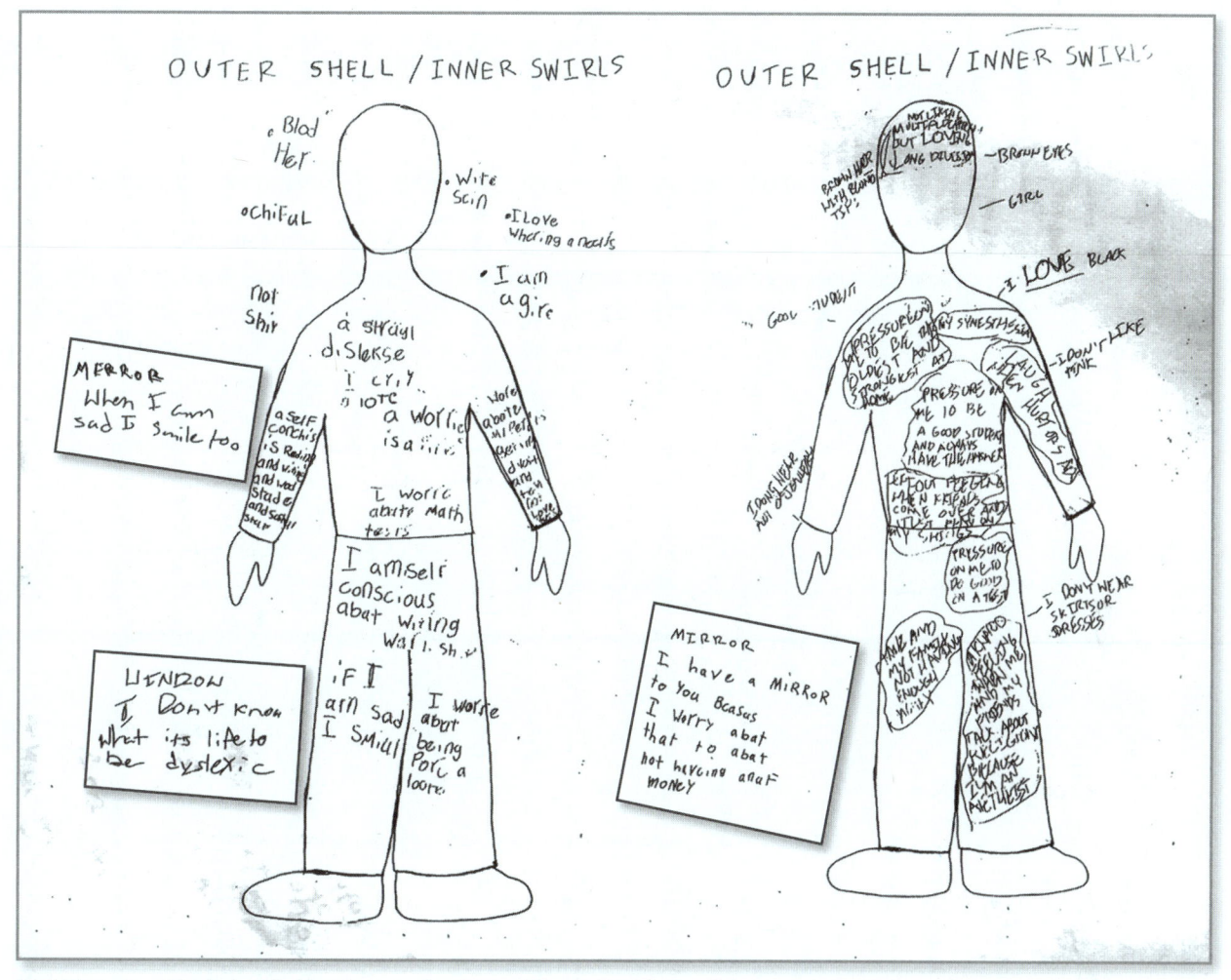

Children can add window/mirror jots to classmates' Outer Shell/Inner Swirls Identity Maps

My student Leah once said, "If you don't share about [your inner swirls], then no one else will have a mirror." We *all* need mirrors, particularly for inner swirls that we worry belong to us alone.

Take the example above. These students discovered unexpected mirrors in each other: Both children sometimes worry about not having enough money, and both sometimes mask their true feelings with a smile. Identifying these mirrors was a deeply comforting, validating experience for these children. By sharing about their inner lives and naming the mirrors and windows they found in each other, they opened themselves up to receive support—from each other, from teachers or counselors, and from their grown-ups at home.

PART 1: Establish and Maintain a Connected Classroom Community

# Curricular Connections

Apply the language across subject areas with these ideas.

**Individual Reflection Exercise: What Mirrors Are You Itching For?**

Ask students to write briefly about what "mirrors of themselves" they would like to see more of in books, movies, or TV. (See More Mirrors, Please! template, below.) Their responses can help you cultivate a more inclusive classroom library—and get to know your students better, too.

(left) From a former student: "I am dyslexic and I want to see me in movies. . . . I'm saying this for every kid with dyslexia."

(below) Another student hopes to see more boy main characters who wear glasses.

See page 133 for this reproducible template.

44

The Words That Shape Us

**Reading Response: Window/Mirror Jots and Silent Conversation**

Window/mirror language is an especially powerful tool for facilitating students' engagement with literature. Of reading, education professor Rudine Sims Bishop (1990) writes: "Children need windows and mirrors. They need mirrors in which they see themselves and windows through which they see the world." As older students read independently, they can look for windows and mirrors and jot down their discoveries in their reading notebooks. Younger students can draw window/mirror symbols (and include words, if they'd like) on sticky notes, posting them directly onto the pages of picture books.

A practice that both younger and older kids enjoy is jotting down window/mirror reactions on different colored sticky notes in a "silent conversation"—one child reads and marks up the book with their window/mirror reactions, and then a second child reads and responds. The students reflect: How were their experiences of the same book similar and different?

A prekindergartner responds to *A Big Mooncake for Little Star* by drawing a window and saying, "I have never made a mooncake before."

Window/mirror jots in response to *I Dissent*, a picture book about Ruth Bader Ginsburg

PART 1: Establish and Maintain a Connected Classroom Community

## Partnering With Families

Share these strategies with families for weaving the language into their home lives.

### Families can weave window/mirror language into conversations at home.

| | |
|---|---|
| **PARENT:** | The way you do math at school is a window for me—I learned math in a different way, so I have a lot to learn from you. Can you teach me how to draw ten sticks? |

| | |
|---|---|
| **PARENT:** | Are there any window or mirror books you wish we had at home? We can go look at the library! |
| **NOVA:** | Yes—the window of being a triplet! Jack is a triplet, and he always has people to play with. But I also think sharing is hard. Let's ask if there are any books about that. |

| | |
|---|---|
| **PARENT:** | You're right to notice that your classmate has two dads, while you have a mom and a dad. Her family structure is a window in that way. But we also have a mirror to her family, because her dads love her just as your father and I love you, and they tuck her in at night and play all sorts of silly games with her, too. Like you, she's surrounded by warm, cozy love. |

### Families can bring mirror books into the classroom as a part of a "mystery reader" tradition.

My co-teacher Anneliese introduced me to one of my favorite classroom traditions ever: inviting a "mystery reader" parent or special grown-up to swing by the classroom and read a picture book of their choice. (These mystery readers might appear every other Friday, and those who are unable to visit in person can do so virtually. By the end of the year, every child experiences a special grown-up reading to the class.) The Sunday before the mystery reader's visit, the parent emails five clues about their identity to the classroom teacher, who shares one clue per day with students (to their great delight). On Friday, the mystery reader's identity is revealed.

A teacher recently shared with me that she adapted this mystery-reader practice by asking parents to choose a picture book that mirrors something about them or about their family. After the read-aloud, children share the windows and mirrors that they, in turn, discovered in the visitor's book. This adaptation is a wonderful way to make space for all that parents bring to your classroom community.

## BRAIN-CHANGING WORDS
## *"I love how/I felt/I never knew ___"*

To me, one of the strangest things about school is how often children's gorgeous work goes straight from the child to the teacher (for the teacher to evaluate in isolation) instead of being experienced and celebrated within the broader classroom community. When we create space for kids to share their work with one another, and when we explicitly teach children how to respond to their peers' contributions in specific ways, student engagement soars. Kids know that they're creating work in a meaningful context, so they're more invested in assignments. Most crucially, when students reflect on their peers' feedback about how the work in question inspired, surprised, or moved them, they discover that they have the power to create things that *matter*—things that initiate connection and change.

The power of peer-to-peer feedback hit home for me when my student Charlotte stood in front of the class and read aloud a tribute she'd written about her classmate Eleanor. Inspired by Margaret Wise Brown's *The Important Book*, Charlotte listed a few important things to know about her friend: She wrote about Eleanor's deep capacity for kindness, her love of art, and her remarkable work ethic. Eleanor, recently diagnosed with dyslexia, was indeed an exceptionally hard worker. She labored over her writing with a focus and determination that floored me and my co-teacher Casey. After Charlotte finished reading aloud, she reached over into the center of the rug where Eleanor sat cross-legged and handed her the tribute. Suddenly, Eleanor burst into tears. Charlotte scrambled over her classmates to hug her friend, and Eleanor said, "You see me the way I want to see myself." Just as the children had wiggled their fingers in Leo's direction to send him love throughout his mirror-book share, all hands shot up to send love to Eleanor, who was beaming through her tears and holding her tribute tight. And while the moment was momentous for Eleanor, it was equally important for Charlotte, who had just discovered how powerful her words could be.

> **When we create space for kids to share their work with one another, and when we explicitly teach children how to respond to their peers' contributions in specific ways, student engagement soars.**

Eleanor took home her tribute that day, and I'd bet she still has it. There's something special about being able to hold on to authentic, specific feedback from someone else, to turn the paper over in your hands and revisit it. That feeling resists digitization—we carefully store and reread handwritten notes but rarely return to old emails. And while kids can't take home a personalized tribute every day (though I highly recommend an "important thing" tribute exchange; see page 53), we *can* give children language that empowers them to give meaningful feedback to one another. They can use the "I love how/I felt/I never knew" feedback protocol anytime in conversation or via jots collected into special booklets that kids can take home and keep indefinitely. I recommend using this second format sparingly, in the context of a formal celebration of student work, like a publishing party or culminating social studies project.

PART 1: Establish and Maintain a Connected Classroom Community

## Introducing This Language

Below, I've outlined how you might introduce "I love how/I felt/I never knew" language as both verbal and written feedback. (If you choose to try both, be sure to introduce the verbal format before the written format.) More than any other language suggestion, this feedback protocol inspires infinite variation. Kids love building upon these words with supportive language of their own.

### Verbal Feedback

Try a version of this:

**MS. LILY:** This classroom is brimming with your one-of-a-kind contributions. As you experience each other's work, it's important to tell one another how the work moves and inspires you. One of the neatest things about being human is that we can dream things into being that live outside of our brains—let's say, a sketch of an imaginary creature—and that sketch can trigger a brand-new idea within *someone else's* brain (a total stranger across the ocean, even). In this classroom, your contributions will surprise and influence one another all the time. Giving and receiving thoughtful, specific feedback can help us all better understand how our work lives and breathes in this classroom in impactful, wonderful ways.

Today, we're going to try out the "I love how/I felt/I never knew" feedback protocol. Joanna has volunteered to share her writer's notebook cover under the document camera as we try this out. Joanna, will you share about the photos and illustrations that you decided to glue onto your cover?

**JOANNA:** I love watermelon, so I glued this picture on. And my totally wild little brother puts peanut butter in his hair just to be funny, so I drew that here. And once my older sister took this picture of me reading under the covers with this flashlight after bedtime, because I just can't stop reading even when I'm supposed to. Also, red pandas are the cutest animals in the world. To me.

**MS. LILY:** Thank you, Joanna. Listen to how I use these sentence stems to respond to Joanna's share, referencing the suggestions on this anchor chart: *Joanna,* ***I love how*** *you drew a picture of your family in addition to including a photograph. The chunks of peanut butter you included in your brother's hair really made me laugh. When you were talking about how you like to read under the covers with a flashlight and showed us that photo,* ***I felt*** *like I was secretly reading, too, excited and a bit nervous I'd get caught. My stomach even got flippy. And* ***I never knew*** *that you love red pandas so much. I have a mirror to you!*

# Kids' Turn

**MS. LILY:** Your turn: You can use any of these stems to respond to Joanna's share and, of course, include your own supportive language, too.

**ROMAN:** I love how your eyes sort of twinkled when you talked about how wild and funny your brother can be.

**POPPY:** When you showed the photo of you biting into that enormous watermelon, I felt really curious because I've never bitten directly into a watermelon. That's a window for me. Was it heavy?

**NORA:** I never knew you were such a funny drawer.

Consider creating an anchor chart, like the one below, for students to refer to when providing both verbal and written feedback.

---

**When giving feedback to a peer, consider:**

"I love how . . ."
- What gives you a vivid mind movie?
- What captures your attention?
- What intrigues/delights you?

"I felt . . ."
- What is happening in your body as you look at/listen to your classmate's work?
- What inspires you?
- What do you want to know more about?

"I never knew . . ."
- What assumptions were interrupted?
- What windows/mirrors do you find?
- What surprises you?

**Written Option**

**MS. LILY:** Today, to celebrate the poems you've chosen to read aloud to the class, we're going to use "I love how/I felt/I never knew" language in a new way—not out loud, but instead in brief notes we jot down as we reflect on each poetry performance. I'm going to collect the notes and staple them into small booklets—mementos that brim with all the ideas and connections that your poems inspired. Of course, as you listen, please jot down any other loving language of your own that comes to mind, too. Specificity wins the day!

---

synesthesia
By Harper

i have
synesthesia
i have
constant colors
blurring
my vision
i have
words
blooming
booming
with color
in my brain
i feel the words
as
i read them
my eyes
shoot
past the page
colors
blinding me
cutting me
burning me
and comforting me
all
at once

---

a blanket
lying on top of me
slashed away
by
the cutting
hacking
my skin
and
a brilliant flash
of orange
and purple
then
a green slash
i feel
slashing
i see
green
and
the world
is covered
in
a thick
blanket
with all my colors
twisted into
the fabric
and
i feel

---

see
and know
all
at once
synesthesia
is
all
of me
and I
am all
of it
if i were a turtle
it would be my shell
if i were a butterfly
it would be my wings
and
all the colors
aren't there
when the book closes
the colors exist
in my head only
the colors
belong
to me
synesthesia
swirling
inside
me.

---

Dear Harper,
Your poem made me feel physically your description of synesthesia. Your brain is incredible!
Love,
Anneliese

Dear Harper, you did a good job putting the metaphors, and while you read it - I could see colors zooming in my brain.
Love,
Leah

Dear Harper, I love when you say "colors bliding me comfuding me" so amazing Harper! you are a true poet
Love, Indira

Harper's classmates respond to her poem about synesthesia, a perceptual phenomenon that enables Harper to associate letters with colors.

The Words That Shape Us

**Disabled**

You might think I'm
100% blind
and I do not know how to learn
"right"

Just because I'm disabled
You think you can win every battle

Just because I can't see right
doesn't mean I'm an idiot

Just because I've done crazy things with my glasses on
doesn't mean I couldn't see what I was doing

Just because I have been disabled
for so long

Does not mean
I have never been a good student.

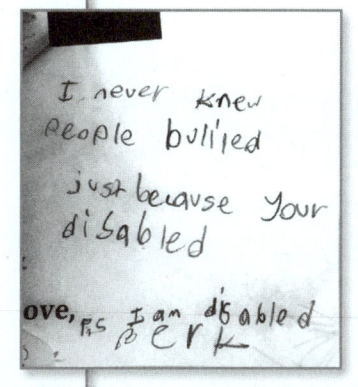

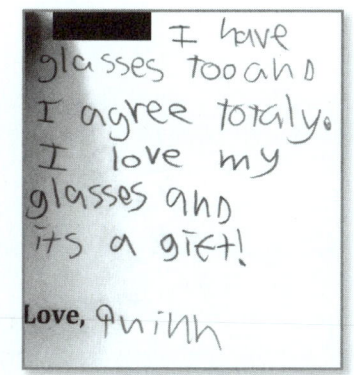

---

*I never knew people bullied just because your disabled*
*Love, P.S. I am disabled Berk*

*I have glasses too and I agree totaly. I love my glasses and its a gift!*
*Love, Quinn*

*I like how you show how your not weak at all*
*Love, Julian*

---

Note the power of a mirror: After this child shared his poem about being disabled (above), Berk—a new student in the class—shared with the author that he, too, is disabled—"P.S., I am disabled." And about the author's language: Although many teachers prefer to say "learning variation" or "has a disability," *disabled* is the language that resonated with this child. Whenever possible, student language and adaptations should lead the way.

---

**You Think I'm...(Part 2 of My Dyslexic Brain)**
By Tirzah

I may not be good at memorizing math facts
But when you see a playground, I see a magical forest

I may not be good at word study
But put me on a stage
and I'll perform a great show

You might just look at the stars and think
"Look at those boring stars, they're useless!"
But I look at the stars
And see a whole world worth exploring

You might look at the ocean and think
"It's just an ocean, what's the point?"
But I see another whole world worth discovering

---

*Tirzah, Love that when I see a playgrond I see a wonderlnd you are asome and ishfulley*

*Tirzah, you have a very good good good good Brain a very good Dislexsiay Brain.*
*Love, Samuel PS321*

Tirzah's poem, which she dictated, and her classmates' responses (right)

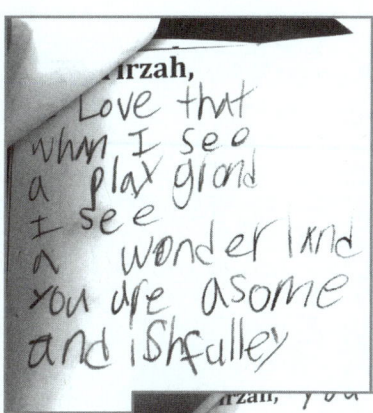

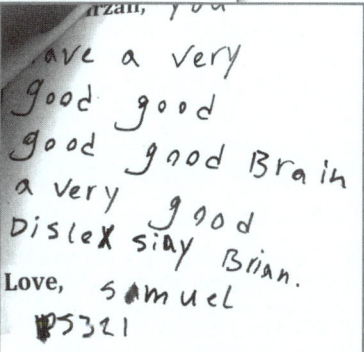

PART 1: Establish and Maintain a Connected Classroom Community

Again, how kids feel at school is tethered to how they do at school. My student Tirzah's experience of receiving a feedback booklet in response to her poem "You Think I'm . . ." (page 51) illustrates this truth. Tirzah, an incredibly bright, creative child, would occasionally become so frustrated during writing time that she'd lay her head down on her desk and close her eyes tight. Her parents reported that to avoid reading and writing at school the previous year, she would sometimes hide under her bed in the morning. After Tirzah received the feedback booklet, Anneliese and I noticed a marked change in her perception of herself as a writer. Her classmates' support helped her identify as an extraordinary poet—and rightfully so. Tirzah jumped into writing assignments with determination and a desire to express herself. She became more open to using accommodations, such as speech-to-text and working with an interventionist. And though the next year Tirzah transitioned to a specialized school for students with dyslexia, she entered her new school with the understanding that her creative strengths exist *because of,* not *in spite of*, her neurodivergence, and with a confident sense of her own "very good good good brain, a very good dyslexic brain," as her classmate Samuel reminded her.

Younger children can draw hearts next to aspects of a classmate's work that they're drawn to or curious about and then tell each other *why* they drew hearts there. (This exercise is especially successful in partnerships.) This prekindergartner said, "I love the fire coming out of the tentacles so I drew a heart there. And I love the sharp beak so I drew a heart there, too."

Some administrators feel that, given the amount of curriculum that must be covered, there simply isn't time for students to offer feedback to one another in this way. But when it comes to "covering curriculum," here's the thing (to borrow a familiar phrase): *Just because we teach it doesn't mean they learned it.* As a new teacher, I'd deliver a zippy mini-lesson to a group of seemingly attentive children and think, "Check!" Then, as I conferenced with students, I'd discover that a child had been daydreaming about colossal squids and hadn't caught a word of the lesson (which was, no doubt, less engaging than contemplating giants of the deep). Years ago, a student said, "Sometimes I look like I'm listening, but I get into the rowboat in my head and row away to a more interesting place." I'm convinced that much of what we think we teach children—especially the sort of explicit instruction that's delivered from the front of the classroom, not tethered to students' unique interests or priorities—doesn't actually land. Or it lands ever so briefly, but it doesn't stick: Kids might learn something new, regurgitate it on an assessment, then promptly forget it.

The teaching profession is bound to transform in ways we can't yet imagine, thanks to flexible access to information, blended learning, and artificial intelligence. I think we need to reframe our jobs as less about solely instilling information and more about facilitating moments that positively transform how kids see themselves and their potential. Moments like Tirzah's experience of reading her poem aloud and receiving tangible feedback from her peers. Moments filled with language that inspires children to tell new stories about their abilities, which in turn empowers them to navigate challenges with resilience and hope.

## Curricular Connection

Apply the language across subject areas with this idea.

### Tribute Exchange: Important Thing

Because children can't keep secrets—nor should they!—I suggest introducing this special tribute exchange on either a December or June afternoon (right before school lets out for winter or summer break), and the kids can write their tributes then and there in class. First, read aloud *The Important Book*, by Margaret Wise Brown, and tell children that they'll be honoring each other using a similar structure. Then, you can whisper the name of a friend to each child. Using the "Important Thing" Planner (page 134), children can draft their tributes.

Margaret Wise Brown's *The Important Book* is a wonderful mentor text for this tribute exchange.

One language shift, inspired by a parent's suggestion: Instead of using Brown's exact language, try: *To me, an important thing about you is* ___. This shift reminds the recipient that whatever lovely thing their friend writes is subjective and one of *many* important things. After you glance at drafts to ensure they're kind and appropriate, children can publish their tributes on colorful construction paper and decorate them however they like. At the end of the day, students present the tributes to one another.

**"Important Thing" Planner**

Think about this person's idiosyncrasies, interests, and strengths. How can you make them feel truly known and celebrated?

(Person's name)

To me, an important thing about you is _____

It is true that you _____

It is true that you _____

It is true that you _____

But to me, an important thing about you is _____

See page 134 for this reproducible template.

**Emilio**

To me, an important thing about you is that you have a kind heart

It is true you have a way with words
It is true you love the Beatles
It is true you love to find a cozy corner and read
It is true you can impersonate any character

But to me, an important thing about you is that you have a kind heart

This exercise can be easily adapted for younger students. Children can collectively create an "Important Thing" tribute to their classroom community, verbally volunteering lines that the teacher records, like the one below.

*To us, the important thing about our classroom community is that we take care of one another:*

It is true we pretend to be spies in the hallway

It is true we make up silly songs

It is true we wish quiet time was longer

It is true we make the tallest structures

It is true teddy grahams are our favorite snack

It is true we feel all our feelings

It is true we like to paint our feet

It is true we think peregrine falcons are the coolest

*But to us, the important thing about our classroom community is that we take care of one another.*

# Partnering With Families

Share these strategies with families for weaving this language into their home lives.

**Families can use this language to give feedback to children.**

"I love how/I felt/I never knew" language can help parents move away from "Good job!" and toward more process-oriented, specific feedback when responding to their children's at-home creations, performances, and the like. "I never knew," in particular, helps parents send the important message that their children brim with all sorts of wonderful surprises that are lovingly accepted and celebrated within the family unit.

PARENT: (looking at a child's sketch of Athena) I never knew that you were so interested in Greek mythology. I love how I can learn about this from you. Tell me about Athena!

PARENT: (after a child's performance) I felt so happy for you as I watched you up there! You were beaming. I never knew how much joy performing brings you. I'm so glad to know this now.

**Families can bring their own feedback language and routines to the classroom.**

One child shared with the class that whenever she shows her mother a block structure or a piece of artwork, her mother doesn't share her favorite part but instead asks, "What is *your* favorite part?" Before long, this question became a popular refrain as students reacted to one another's choice-time creations.

Honoring how families share feedback with one another is a great way to incorporate home language and rituals into your classroom community.

# PART 2
# Cultivate Students' Self-Awareness, Self-Compassion, and Self-Regulation

Complete self-understanding isn't possible. Corners of our inner lives may always remain mysteries: Why does someone's presence annoy us when they've never done anything to antagonize us? Why do we feel compelled to say yes to every request, even when we're stretched too thin? Nobel Prize–winning psychologist and economist Daniel Kahneman (2013) teaches us that, often, the reason we give for why we felt or did something is not the *real* reason, but a rationale we've come up with imperceptibly quickly after the fact. The actual reason is unconscious, instinctive, influenced by an enormous variety of subtle factors. Take the smell of a particular space: A study by psychologist Simone Schnall (2008) and her colleagues reveals that when people sit in a foul-smelling, messy room, their judgments of moral offensives (such as lying and stealing) are harsher than those of individuals who sit in a lovely-smelling room. In-the-moment unconscious cues, like odor or the orderliness of a particular space, affect what we say and do all the time. But most of our behaviors and knee-jerk reactions are rooted in hazy, hard-to-pin-down core beliefs that were formed long ago, during the most important phase of our lives, neurobiologically speaking: our childhoods.

> **Most of our behaviors and knee-jerk reactions are rooted in hazy, hard-to-pin-down core beliefs that were formed long ago . . . in our childhoods.**

Decades of research support the truth that our experiences and attachments as children—particularly between birth and age 8, when our brains develop most rapidly (CDC, 2017)—draft the blueprints that can structure our thoughts and actions for the rest of our lives. Setting significant childhood trauma[1] or neglect aside, many of the run-of-the-mill unhealthy tendencies that plague reasonably

---

[1] Childhood trauma can lead to the development of a larger, hyperactive amygdala and poor frontal-cortex development, which in turn leads to poor emotional regulation and impulse control. It is unsurprising, then, that most people who commit violent crimes experienced childhood adversity (Sapolsky, 2017).

well-adjusted people are simply maladaptive behaviors that were once adaptive (Schwartz, 2021). People-pleasing, perfectionism, conflict avoidance, a tendency to overcontrol—these behaviors are hard to shed because they're trying to *keep doing their jobs*. After all, these strategies served children well when they needed to keep the peace with the sometimes-volatile, micromanaging, or emotionally removed caregivers who were responsible for keeping them fed and safe. As self-sufficient adults, it takes a whole lot of metacognition (and often years of therapy) to identify these maladaptive behaviors, to thank them for their years of service, and to bid them farewell.

On the flipside, adults who seek out and thrive in steady, loving relationships; who assume the best about others; who speak up for their needs in a regulated, clear way—these individuals typically received consistent care and responsiveness from at least one grown-up during their formative years: "Consistent, nurturing caregivers build an internal view that people are safe, predictable, and caring. . . . We project what we expect, and that helps elicit what we expect" (Perry & Winfrey, 2021). The difficult or wonderful news (and for many, it's a mix of both) is that childhood matters. Our experiences as children don't *ensure* any particular behavior or outcome, but they have tremendous *influence* over the likelihood of certain behaviors or outcomes (Sapolsky, 2017).

So, if our interior worlds are complex and difficult to understand, and if our experiences as children carry implications for the rest of our lives, what does this mean for teachers? I believe that elementary school educators have a unique opportunity to become responsive, caring grown-ups in their students' lives because they spend *so much time* with them. Children in prekindergarten through fifth grade spend approximately 1,000 hours with the same teacher or co-teaching team in a "home-base" classroom each year. These positive student-teacher connections alone can work wonders. But elementary school educators can do something else, too: Because their students are typically less

Elementary school teachers have an unusual amount of time to form responsive, supportive relationships with their students.

Part 2: Cultivate Students' Self-Awareness, Self-Compassion, and Self-Regulation

self-conscious and peer-focused than middle- or high-school students, teachers will find that these younger children are often more receptive to, and more able to experiment with, language that helps them positively navigate their inner lives. And while knowing themselves will be a life-long journey and never fully possible, the right words can open the door to understanding a great deal of why and how they think, and this language can empower kids to *choose what to pay attention to* within their own minds.

We become what we pay attention to (Wu, 2016). When a child gives their full attention to a worry about being left behind at recess, they can experience nausea and paralysis, refusing to head outside to the yard. But when this child directs their attention to the phrase, *Remember—just because I think it doesn't make it true,* they can direct their minds somewhere else, somewhere healthier, and make a better decision. In other words, kids have more agency than they realize when it comes to how they feel and what they think. I love what David Foster Wallace had to say about this in his 2005 commencement address at Kenyon College, "This Is Water":

> Learning how to think means learning how to exercise some control over how and what you think. It means being conscious and aware enough to choose what you pay attention to and to choose how you construct meaning from experience.[2]

Words are tools for regulating human minds and bodies (Barrett, 2017). And access to the right "tools" can help children determine which thoughts or impulses to amplify and which ones to quiet. The language in this section will help students move through their school days with increased self-awareness, self-compassion, and self-regulation (skills that are closely tethered to academic and social success). And beyond school, the language in this section simply helps children's minds become kinder, more joyful places to reside.

---

[2] Tragically, Wallace suffered from severe depression and died by suicide in 2008. His wisdom and prescience in this much-beloved graduation address (the only public talk he gave about his views on living) are extraordinary. Especially in this attention economy, Wallace's words underscore the importance of deliberate mindfulness and self-compassion.

## 🗨 BRAIN-CHANGING WORDS

# *"Hello, feeling visitor!"*
# *"You are separate from your feeling."*

Individuals with greater emotional granularity—essentially, a larger emotional vocabulary—have greater psycho-social well-being and are poised for greater academic success (David, 2016; Brackett, 2019). Naming feelings with precision and nuance not only helps us better tailor our emotional experiences to certain situations but also underscores the truth that *feelings are impermanent*. It's a whole lot easier to notice that our emotional experiences are constantly shifting if we have language to describe those shifts.

That notion that our feelings are like guests within us, not permanent residents, might seem obvious to an adult. But it's not at all obvious to a child who feels the urge to hide behind a tree at a track meet, a voice inside shouting, *You'll humiliate yourself if you lose*, and a wave of inadequacy washing over him. The phrases "Hello, feeling visitor!" and "You are separate from your feeling" empower this student to take a step back and realize that the feeling of inadequacy is simply something he's experiencing, not who he is. The "visitor" language is inspired by my favorite Rumi poem, "The Guest House" (right).

> **The Guest House** by Jalaluddin Rumi (excerpt)
>
> This being human is a guest house. Every morning a new arrival.
>
> A joy, a depression, a meanness, some momentary awareness comes as an unexpected visitor.

When we remind children that feelings are like visitors—by asking, "What feelings visited you this morning on your walk to school?" or observing, "I see your head is on your desk. What feeling is visiting you right now? Remember: You are separate from your feeling"—we help children develop emotional granularity while also reinforcing the truth that their identities are separate from their emotional experiences. This delineation decreases shame and increases honesty. It's easier to share about a difficult feeling if you don't feel like that feeling is an unflattering reflection of your core self.

Some children will immediately adopt the term "feeling visitor," while others will prefer to keep using "feeling." Both work well, and there's no need to standardize the language. Simply introducing the visitor metaphor[3] helps children consider the impermanence of their emotional experiences. As students share about their inner lives, it's important to receive whatever they contribute without judgment and to share accordingly with parents and counselors. (I always preview with kids that the safe, loving grown-ups in their lives will share relevant information with one another and work together to support them.) All feeling visitors, even difficult ones, have something to teach us, perhaps about a repressed hope or about something we care deeply about but have no control over. Take anger, an emotion concept far richer and more complex than we might realize. Poet David Whyte (2021)

---

3 This metaphor is not perfect. Feelings are not exactly like visitors because, as I've touched upon, emotions don't *happen* to us, we *construct* them. That said, it sure doesn't feel that way: A tidal wave of envy or resentment can seem to take us by surprise and bowl us over. Comparing feelings to visitors is empowering for kids because it helps them view their emotional experiences with an awareness of their ephemerality and with more distance, curiosity, and agency.

writes: "What we have named as anger on the surface is the violent outer response to our own inner powerlessness, powerlessness connected to such a profound sense of rawness and care that it can find no proper outer body or identity or voice." When a child expresses rage, it's important to investigate the powerlessness or deep caring *beneath* the outburst.

When children try to make sense of their most challenging or nuanced emotions, words often fail them or bring them only halfway to the truth. But the richer a child's emotional vocabulary, and the more comfortable that child feels discussing their interior life, the closer they'll get to what they really mean. And as they—or you—grapple with challenging feeling visitors, I find it helpful to remember Rumi's advice in the third stanza of "The Guest House": "Treat each guest honorably / He may be clearing you out for some new delight."

To be clear, treating each guest honorably does not mean encouraging children to wallow in difficult emotions. Instead, it means inviting kids to *name* the feeling so it doesn't curdle within them, inhibiting the openness and risk-taking that lead to cognitive growth. Brené Brown (2021) reminds us that, paradoxically, naming a hard emotional experience "doesn't give the experience more power, it gives us the power of understanding and meaning."

Finally, in addition to fostering self-awareness, this language inspires children to embrace a more nuanced understanding of their peers' behavior. When a child pushes a chair in frustration, a fellow student who has internalized the "you are separate from your feeling" ethos understands that their classmate is not "bad" but simply struggling to regulate. This is a radical shift in perception that empowers children to move away from asking, "What is wrong with you?" and toward asking, "What about this is hard for you?"—an infinitely more productive approach to navigating others' challenging behavior (and one we'll explore in depth on page 111).

## Introducing This Language

I like to introduce these two phrases together ("Hello, feeling visitor!" and "You are separate from your feeling") in the context of a morning-message discussion question, like the one at right, and accompanying personal anecdote. I typically project morning messages on an interactive whiteboard, but many teachers prefer to write them on chart paper. If a morning message is not a part of your daily routine, you can introduce the language during any class meeting or reflection time.

---

April 3rd

**Dear Second Graders:**

We've got lots of wonderful things ahead today: a visit from Aidan's grandmother, a brand-new math game to learn, and you'll be observing and sketching real worms (!) in art class.

This morning's discussion question is below:

**What feeling visitors stopped by your mind on your way to school this morning?**

Here's to another beautiful day of learning together—

Lily & Casey

Try a version of this:

**MS. LILY:** Before you answer this question, I'd like to pause and share a bit about the unusual phrase you see here: "feeling visitors."

Please give me a mirror signal if you've ever felt so frustrated you thought you might explode. I know I have. Everyone has! When I was a kid, my friend Annie's sister would play a terrible trick on her: She'd hide Annie's shoes. This drove Annie bonkers; she would scream and scream. She didn't say, "I feel frustrated," because she didn't know that word. She would just lie down and keep on yelling. Here's what Annie's dad told her: "You are separate from your feeling. Frustration is visiting you, but it's not *who you are*. When you say, 'I feel frustrated' and explain what's bothering you, I can help."

Annie's dad helped her understand that feelings are like visitors: They come and go. Annie learned that if she could name her feeling—frustration—then she could see it clearly and not feel so overtaken by it, as if an alien had inhabited her body and was making her yell and flail! With her dad's help, Annie calmed down and explained to her sister why she was so frustrated by the shoe-hiding trick.

All feelings are visitors inside us—none of them stay forever. And when we name our feelings, we understand what's happening inside us just a little bit better.

Now, back to this discussion question. Raise a hand if you'd like to share about a few feeling visitors that swung by your mind on your way to school this morning.

**ISABELLA:** I felt so, so hopeful when I saw the ice-cream truck parked around the corner from my dad's house!

**GRAYSON:** A super-annoyed feeling visited me on the train when I realized that my little sister had picked the marshmallow parts out of my dry cereal.

**CAMILA:** When my babysitter played my favorite song in the car on the way to school, I yelled because I felt so excited. Excitement visits me a lot when I'm with my babysitter because she's so fun and funny.

# Kids' Turn

Here are some ways children can use and internalize this language.

- In the context of a morning-meeting game, children can take turns standing in front of the group and inhabiting the voice of any feeling visitor they'd like—boredom, joy, disgust, and so on—saying, "Oh hello, here I am!" in the tone and physicality of the emotion. (Slow and sluggish for boredom; bubbly for excitement. This game is a hit and elicits lots of giggles.) As classmates guess emotion words, you can add them to a feeling-visitor vocabulary bank, organized by colors that align with the Yale Center for Emotional Intelligence Mood Meter (see sidebar). Referencing this bank not only increases children's emotional granularity but also empowers them to use rich language in their creative writing and reading responses.

- In pairs or small groups, children can name the feelings that visited them throughout a shared class experience (such as a field trip), offering window/mirror feedback:

    **SYBIL:** When I saw the snow leopard, fear and excitement visited me at the same time. I wanted to get super close to it, and I wanted to run away.

    **IAN:** I have a window to you because when I saw the snow leopard, I felt all warm and cozy. The leopard reminded me of my cat, and I wanted to cuddle it. I didn't feel nervous at all!

**Feeling Visitor Word Bank**

Livid
Frustrated
Peeved

Suprised
nervous

Delighted
Playful
Ecstatic
Proud

Glum
Drained
Bored
Sad

Serene
calm
Satisfied
cozy

The beginning stages of a Feeling Visitor Word Bank. (Teachers of young kids can use simpler language and visual cues, such as sketching a face next to each word.) As the chart paper becomes full, simply attach chart paper on either side to extend the categories horizontally.

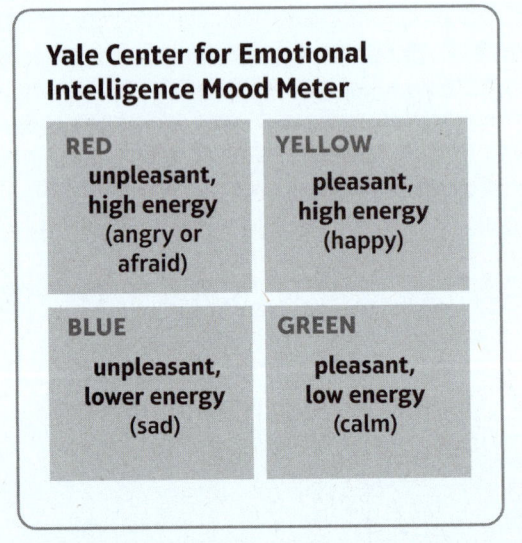

**Yale Center for Emotional Intelligence Mood Meter**

| RED<br>unpleasant, high energy (angry or afraid) | YELLOW<br>pleasant, high energy (happy) |
|---|---|
| BLUE<br>unpleasant, lower energy (sad) | GREEN<br>pleasant, low energy (calm) |

For more information about the color-coded mood meter, go to: scholastic.com/ourbestselves/pdfs/our_best_selves-lessons_1.pdf

- Teachers can elicit suggestions from children to create a self-talk anchor chart, like the one below.

> **Difficult feeling visitors and impulses popping by to say hello?**
>
> When I feel like I want to push someone, I can remind myself:
>
> * I am separate from this impulse. I can make a better choice.
>
> When I feel sad, I can remind myself:
>
> * Everyone feels sadness sometimes, and sadness is an important part of being a human being. Naming and sharing about sadness help me understand it.
>
> When I feel like I'll stay annoyed and/or angry forever, I can remind myself:
>
> * No feeling is permanent.

## Curricular Connections

Apply the language across subject areas with these ideas.

### Reading Response: Big Event → Feeling Visitor

Big events invite all sorts of feeling visitors—for characters in the books we read *and* for ourselves. This simple, weblike reading response encourages children to imagine and name feelings that might visit characters in the wake of big events. It also sets the stage for children to name and consider their emotional responses to big events in their own lives.

In Sophie Blackall's *Hello Lighthouse*, a lighthouse keeper and his family live in a lighthouse. Their home is cramped, yes, but also cozy and chock-full of wonder. One day, the keeper receives a letter saying that an automatic light will be installed: His job is obsolete. Below, I model imagining and jotting down the feelings that might visit the keeper as he considers the arrival of the automatic light. (Older kids can easily sketch a Big Event → Feeling Visitor web in their reading notebooks.)

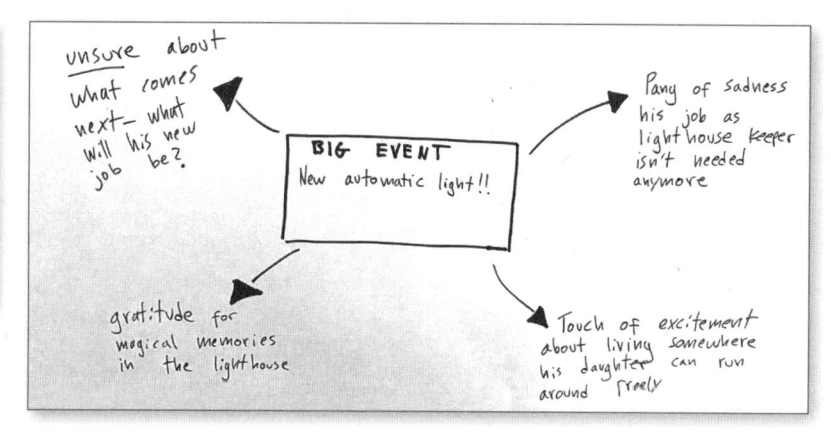

Part 2: Cultivate Students' Self-Awareness, Self-Compassion, and Self-Regulation

In Cozbi A. Cabrera's *Me & Mama*, a girl and her mother spend a joyful rainy day together. Below, a prekindergartner draws a picture of a big event in the story: the girl splashing in a puddle, which he labels "PDL." He also draws and labels two of the character's feeling visitors in that moment: "HP" (happy) and "SE" (silly).

**Poetry Invitation: Feeling Visitors Inside Me**

Poet and teacher Georgia Heard (1999) writes: "It's a poet's job to know the interior of his or her heart." When it comes to encouraging children to name their feeling visitors, poetry can serve as a portal to their inner worlds. After my co-teacher Casey and I both moved away from Washington, D.C., to teach in California and Brooklyn, respectively, Casey inspired her new group of students to write introspective poetry. Her third-grade student Avin shared the reflection below with her.

> The most important lesson that poetry has taught me is how to express myself and my emotions. I have strong emotions and sometimes I just feel like I can't talk to anybody. So, I talk through my poems. I have written poems about my sadness and joy, fear and confidence. This has always made me feel better.
>
> Poetry is a creative outlet. It lets me put my thoughts down on paper. A way for people to see the world through my lens, walk in my shoes, look at my world. It can be a window for me to look through to see another's life or a way to see deeper into myself.

Avin beautifully expresses how writing poetry about his inner life both enables him to "see deeper" into himself and connects him to others. Writing does that: It gives shape to the chaos within us and builds bridges to other people (Bender, 2013). As I mentioned in Part 1, list poems are an especially simple, accessible way to get kids writing poetry about their inner lives. (Georgia Heard's compilation of list poems, *Falling Down the Page: A Book of List Poems*, brims with fantastic mentor texts.) Consider asking kids to write (or draw) a list of the feelings that visit them at particular moments in their lives.

Tirzah's list poem, below, is not about emotions associated with a specific experience but about emotions associated with being alive, generally. (Leave it to children to take a grown-up's suggestion and infuse it with their own magic.) And, as often happens once a child—or anyone—begins writing, the poem begins as one thing (a list) and then morphs into another form entirely. That's another gift of list poems: Because they're so easy to jump into, because children are off and running, all sorts of new ideas come to them as they go.

A prekindergartner draws three feelings that visited him as he enjoyed the neighborhood carnival.

**Feelings**
by Tirzah

inside
me
feelings
have
parties.

stress
anger
disgust
sadness
love
pressure

and there's also
all those ones I don't really know
there are so many I can't name

there's lots and lots of madness

sadness
sadness is born through my ears
it burns into my years
someone says "you're weird"
I run
bye bye

the madness comes from my foot
sometimes when the madness comes up
I scratch the path up my leg

your feelings watch my feelings
my feelings watch your feelings.

Part 2: Cultivate Students' Self-Awareness, Self-Compassion, and Self-Regulation

## Partnering With Families

The cultural normalization of exploring our interior lives (so we can better understand ourselves, interrupt negative patterns, and operate with increased self-awareness and success) is a relatively new phenomenon. There are dozens of popular podcasts and bestselling books about these ideas now, but there certainly weren't 30 years ago. Some parents in your class may not have had space to share their own difficult feelings when they were children, hearing catchphrases such as, "No one likes a sourpuss" or "Go to your room until you stop crying." And when we—teachers or parents—observe children doing what we weren't allowed to do when we were young, we might feel a prick of annoyance and discomfort. The subconscious truth simmering below this response is understandable: *What I'm seeing wasn't safe for me, so it must not be safe for you. Stop.*

This is where the magic of previewing comes in. None of us do our best when we're caught off guard; it's hard to take in new information when we're acting reflexively or defensively. But a heads-up works wonders. As your students begin to develop emotional granularity and become more comfortable naming their feeling visitors, I suggest sending parents an email or newsletter that shares the research behind why naming emotions bolsters inner well-being, self-regulation, and academic success. (If parents would like to explore these ideas further, you might suggest Susan David's *Emotional Agility*.) Proactively framing this work in the context of research and offering actionable at-home extensions preempts misunderstandings and invites collaboration.

Share these strategies with families for weaving the language into their home lives.

### Children can ask their parents about their feeling visitors.

**ZOEY:** When was a time you felt a bunch of different feeling visitors at once?

**PARENT:** When I was going to the hospital to give birth to you, I felt so many things at once. Anticipation, nervousness, deep joy and excitement, and so much gratitude for the doctors and nurses who would help bring you safely into the world.

### Families can weave this language into read-alouds.

**PARENT:** I love Garth Williams's illustration here (in *Charlotte's Web*). What feelings do you think are visiting Fern as she feeds Wilbur with the bottle?

**CHILD:** I think she's feeling relief because she rescued him and he's safe now. And also probably a lot of coziness and love. And awe because she's never cradled a fuzzy little baby pig like that before.

**In challenging moments, parents can remind children that they are separate from their feeling.**

PARENT: I believe that you feel so angry right now. Remember: You are separate from your anger, and you have a choice about how you express it. Please use your words, not just your screaming, to tell me about why you feel angry. Then I can help you.

**Families can share and celebrate emotion concepts from other languages.**

There are many emotion concepts for which English has no words. For example:

- *uitwaaien*, the Dutch word for the invigorating feeling of taking a walk in the wind
- *wabi-sabi*, the Japanese word for the aching melancholy that accompanies an awareness of impermanence
- *gigil*, the Tagalog word for the irresistible urge to cuddle or pinch someone because they're so darn cute

Parents who speak multiple languages can visit the classroom to share and celebrate new emotion concepts and correlating language or pass along this information via an email to the teacher. Some families may invent their own words (or variations on known words) to express an otherwise inexpressible emotion, and these snippets of home language can also be shared and celebrated within the classroom community.

Children and parents can share about their feeling visitors with each other.

### BRAIN-CHANGING WORDS

## "What can your wisest self say back to other thoughts and feelings in your head?"

In Fred Rogers's 1969 memorable testimony before the Senate, he explained that once kids learn that their feelings are mentionable, they learn that their feelings are manageable, too. The concept of a "wisest self" is the most transformative emotional management tool I've ever encountered. Wrapping language around the idea that each of us possesses an inner leader that can choose what to pay attention to in our own minds empowers kids with tremendous agency as they navigate their thoughts, feelings, and impulses.

It's worth repeating: Lisa Feldman Barrett's (2017) groundbreaking research reveals that we are, to a degree, the architects of our own emotional experiences. Emotions aren't hardwired, uncontrollable brain reactions; they're predictions informed by previous actions and experiences. Take the experience of a child who takes note of her churning stomach and hammering heartbeat before delivering a speech at a school assembly. This student might respond to this moment in two ways. She could think, "I feel sick with worry so I might as well walk away and give up. I wouldn't feel this way if I was prepared." Or, she could think, "What would my wisest self tell me? That my pounding heart means I *care* about this, and I should channel this energy into doing my best. I've got this." Barrett calls the latter response "getting butterflies to fly in formation," an energized determination that positively recategorizes the child's physical response to a pressured moment. This recategorization seeds this child's brain to predict differently in the future, triggering a virtuous cycle: The more she responds this way, the more automatic it becomes.

Before encountering wisest-self language, many children simply don't realize that they have this sort of agency within themselves. And given the amount of micromanaging that kids endure, this makes perfect sense. As adults, we underestimate just how often we tell children what to do: Parents tell kids when to go to bed, when to get up, what to eat; teachers tell kids where to sit, where to stand in line, which page they should open their textbooks to. And while many caregivers and educators empower children to make their own choices as often as possible, the truth is that being a kid inherently requires a lot of following directions. (Yes, despite the occasional outraged looks directed my way, my young children *must* wear coats in the wintertime. They *must* take baths.) Kids don't believe they're in control of what happens to them because, most of the time, *they're not*. So it shouldn't come as much of a surprise that, when a child experiences an unproductive thought or impulse, he reacts passively: "Well, this is just one more thing happening to me. I'm filled with an overwhelming urge to bang Arthur over the head with the clipboard . . . so here goes!"

The notion that it's actually completely typical to think all sorts of things and have all sorts of impulses that might not be helpful to us or rooted in truth—and that we each have a wisest self that can help us choose how to navigate our sometimes-cacophonous inner lives—is downright revelatory for children (and many adults, too). Think of a time when you've felt sick with anxiety about a social situation, only to discover that there was no reason to worry.

Neuroscientist and primatologist Robert Sapolsky (2017) explains that many of us have an overdeveloped anticipatory stress response that is maladaptive to modern life. Worrying about a surprise visit from a saber-toothed tiger was adaptive thousands of years ago, but now that we're not in real danger, our brains invent new problems. Our wisest selves can help us interrupt our anxious ruminations by saying something like: *You can quiet this fear, which is likely not rooted in reality, and pay attention to other things.*

Much of what looks like "misbehavior" at school is actually a child who is having a hard time and who hasn't yet learned how to listen to her wisest self. Returning to the theme of the first part of this book: It's a whole lot easier to listen to one's wisest self and make good choices in the context of a connected, inclusive classroom community in which the student feels safe and valued. Only then is this child's frontal cortex available for high-level reasoning, metacognition, and self-regulation: "The frontal cortex makes you do the harder thing when it's the right thing to do. . . . We refrain from hitting the irritating coworker" (Sapolsky, 2017). In disconnected classrooms, a negative feedback loop emerges: A student who feels unwelcome or shamed, whose amygdala is over-activated and whose frontal cortex functioning is inhibited, has a harder time listening to her wisest self and self-regulating. So this child exhibits *more* challenging behavior, which in turn deepens her sense of isolation. Wisest-self language helps students identify and interrupt these destructive cycles.

If this wisest-self language feels a bit "out there" to you, here's the truth: Everyone has conversations in their heads all day long. The earlier we normalize this for kids, the better. I stopped in my tracks when, listening to one of the world's most popular podcasts, *We Can Do Hard Things,* I heard host Glennon Doyle explain how she's just learning to listen to her "wisest self." If she's using this language, millions of adults are now, too. And the implications of wisest-self language for kids, who have far more capacity for neuroplasticity than adults do, are profound. It empowers them to make energized determinations that change how their brains process new information, pointing them toward self-trust and resilience. And what could be better than a world in which more young people are discerning about what they pay attention to, and give credence to, within their own minds? A world in which kids grow into adults who know how to listen to the kindest, wisest parts of themselves?

## Introducing This Language

When I first introduced the concept of a "wisest self" to a group of third graders many years ago, I had not yet learned about Dr. Richard Schwartz's Internal Family Systems (IFS) model, which is rooted in the idea that the mind is multiple and made up of different parts, led by a compassionate core self. While these inner parts might be wounded or protective—for example, the part of us that itches to control everything—Schwartz (2021) emphasizes that no parts are bad; they've just taken on extreme roles within us (for reasons, you guessed it, rooted in our childhood experiences). I wish I'd told my third graders that their inner leader is wise, yes, but also understanding and nonjudgmental. It isn't "snappy" with the thoughts and feelings it encounters; it calmly talks back and makes a decision. When modeling how *your* wisest self speaks, it's important to always use a low-key, regulated tone.

If you're interested in sharing the concept of an inner leader with kids under 6, I suggest the term "inner voice,"[4] as the idea of listening to a voice inside is more concrete than the concept of multiple parts or selves. For kids in first grade and beyond, I prefer "wisest self," but any moniker that resonates with you or your students is great.

Below, I've modeled how you might introduce wisest-self language in the context of a shared-writing exercise, but you can also introduce this language in the context of an interactive read-aloud. I love reading *Piper Chen Sings*, a gorgeous picture book by Phillipa Soo and Maris Pasquale Doran, to children of all ages. Piper overcomes her stage fright by learning to peacefully acknowledge her butterflies—or *húdié*, in Chinese—by whispering "Hello, *húdié*!" to herself. This phrase, which I remind children comes from Piper's wisest self, helps Piper remember that her butterflies often visit her when something exciting lies ahead and empowers her to positively recategorize the physical experience of a churning stomach before her solo performance.

**MS. LILY:** You're getting lots of practice naming feelings that pop by during the day. Now, here's the thing about those visitors—some of them, like worry, might visit us a little too often. And sometimes, we absolutely need to listen to what worry tells us. If I see a car pulling out of a parking spot in a busy shopping center, I *should* listen to the part of myself that is worried about walking in its path, and I *should* stay still until the car pulls away. But occasionally, a worry swings by and tells me something that's actually not true or helpful; for example, that my alarm clock won't work even though I just put new batteries in it. This sort of thing happens in all brains. Raise a hand if you'd like to share about a worry you've experienced that simply wasn't true or helpful.

**NORA:** Once there was an hour wait for a table at the diner, and I felt so worried that if we left and went to the playground, our table would get taken. My worried feeling kept telling me I should wait and stare at the tables. My dad kept saying he'd get a text and it was okay to leave, but I just stayed there and stared. And cried a little, too.

**MS. LILY:** Thank you for sharing that. It's remarkable how strong and sure that worried feeling can be sometimes, even when the worry isn't rooted in truth. It's almost as if the worry feeling is trying to help and simply overdoing it! Now here's the good news: You have a secret power you might not know about. Inside of you, you have a wisest self, a leader of your mind that gets to choose how to navigate your thoughts and feelings. Your wisest self is the most true-to-you, kind, strong voice inside you. And when you learn to listen to it, you feel better on the inside and you make better choices on the outside.

---

[4] A note of caution: My 5-year-old son now uses "inner voice" language all the time, in inspiring and occasionally maddening ways: "Mommy, my inner voice is telling me I should never call someone else 'stupid.'" "Mommy, my inner voice is telling me I am ready for a much, much later bedtime." But as Dr. Rebecca Herschberg (2024) reminds us, it's impossible for kids to both follow their inner compass and be perfectly compliant; to have a strong sense of self and still constantly seek the approval of grown-ups. We've got to pick our poison, so to speak. When a young child's inner voice shares wisdom that is, well, unwise, I've found this language helpful: "You know it's your inner voice when it's telling you to do the best, healthiest thing for you."

**MS. LILY:** Now, back to that worry-feeling visitor: I'd love your help thinking of what my wisest self might say back to a worry that will likely swing by before I give a speech at an upcoming wedding. Here's what I have so far:

> **WORRY:** You might look really unprepared if you forget what you planned to say.
>
> **WISEST SELF:** That's true. You might look a little unprepared. But actually, sometimes when you can't remember what you planned, what you end up saying in the moment is more authentic. Trust yourself. The words will come to you, and it's okay if they aren't the exact words you intended to say.
>
> **WORRY:** Well, what if you forget to say "thank you" to the hosts of the wedding? That would be terrible!
>
> **WISEST SELF:**

**MS. LILY:** Any ideas? What could my wisest self say back?

**LEILANI:** You could just go tell them when you see them afterwards. Say thank you and that you're sorry for forgetting!

**MS. LILY:** Yes! Thank you for that suggestion, I'll write that down now.

All year long, we'll try to listen to our wisest selves. And here's the best news of all: *The more you listen to your wisest self, the easier it becomes.*

## Kids' Turn

Here are some ways children can use and internalize this language.

- In the context of a puppetry exercise, younger children can draw pictures of their wisest selves and different feeling visitors and tape these pictures to craft sticks. Then they can then improvise conversations, such as the following:

    **LOGAN:** Worry says, "You might get left on the playground!" and my wisest self says, "Remember, we do a count-off when we line up, so that definitely won't happen!"

    *"Wisest Self" and "Pressure" puppets*

- When reflecting on challenging moments, older children can use this language to explore and explain why they made the choices they did:

    **NORA:** When everyone was laughing, I guess I felt like I needed to, too. I felt like if I didn't laugh, it would just be so awkward. A part of me, my wisest part, knew it was wrong. But I didn't listen to that part. I'm really sorry.

- Incorporating children's suggestions, you can create a "Things Your Wisest Self Might Say When . . ." self-talk anchor chart, like the one below, to display in the classroom. Over time, wisest-self language becomes so embedded within kids' inner lives that identifying this wise, kind inner voice becomes habitual.

### Things Your Wisest Self Might Say When . . .

| Your thought or feeling: | Your wisest self: |
|---|---|
| "No one wants to play with me." | "I know recess is hard when your best friend is absent. Try assuming the best. Walk up to a group and ask to join in." |
| "I have no idea what to write. Everybody else's pencil is moving. How does everyone else think of good ideas so quickly?" | "You don't have to have a perfect plan to let your pencil lead the way. Just choose an idea without judging it too much, get started, and see what happens!" |
| "I will never, ever understand this math problem!" | "Your brain is getting the exercise it needs to change and grow. In fact, you could never learn anything challenging without experiencing tricky moments like this one!" |

## Curricular Connections

Apply the language across subject areas with these ideas.

### Reading Response: Coaching Characters

In this reading response, children embody a character's wisest self and "coach" the character through difficult moments. (See page 135 for the reproducible Coaching Characters template.) Younger children can verbally contribute ideas in the context of a class-wide reading response (which doubles as a shared-writing exercise) centered around a read-aloud. Older students might complete this exercise independently for homework as they coach a character of their choice.

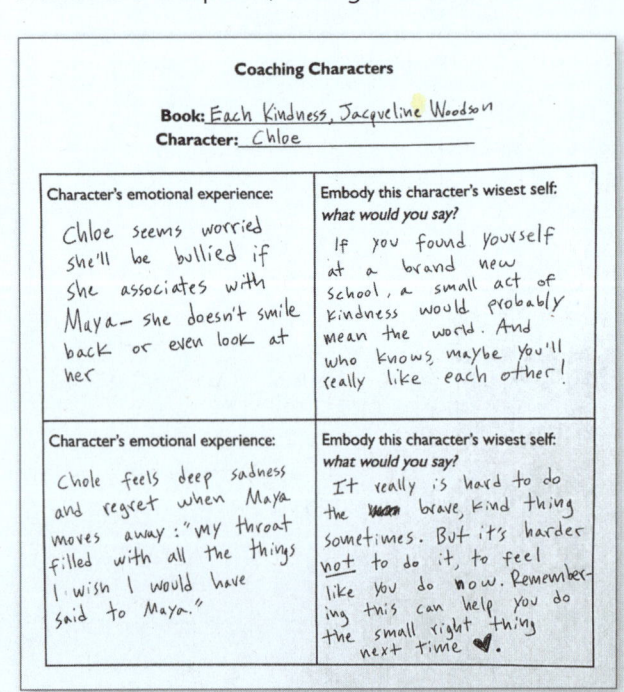

A student imagines herself as the wisest self of Chloe, a character in *Each Kindness*, and offers sage advice.

**Coaching Characters**

Book: Each Kindness, Jacqueline Woodson
Character: Chloe

| Character's emotional experience: | Embody this character's wisest self: what would you say? |
|---|---|
| Chloe seems worried she'll be bullied if she associates with Maya—she doesn't smile back or even look at her. | If you found yourself at a brand new school, a small act of kindness would probably mean the world. And who knows, maybe you'll really like each other! |
| Chloe feels deep sadness and regret when Maya moves away: "my throat filled with all the things I wish I would have said to Maya." | It really is hard to do the brave, kind thing sometimes. But it's harder *not* to do it, to feel like you do *now*. Remembering this can help you do the small right thing next time ♥ |

**Poetry Invitation: Listening to My Wisest Self**

After my third-grade student Harper read aloud her poem "Someone's at the door" (below left), she and her classmates collaboratively brainstormed things that her "President Decider"—her name for her wisest self—could say back to some of her thoughts and feelings, creating a poem for many voices. Though I included Harper's "President Decider" poem in the introduction, it's powerful to see it again next to the poem that inspired it. The two poems paint remarkably different pictures of the same child's inner life and illuminate just how transformative listening to one's inner leader can be.

---

**Someone's at the door**
By Harper

knock
an impatient
rapping
on the front door
of my mind
**pressure**
yells
"OPEN.THE. DOOR."
I reach forward
and open it
pressure is tall
red-faced
with
dark red hair
and
his mouth
is always
open
wide
screeching
noise
always
yelling
I hear his screams
he is yelling
"RAISE YOUR HAND HIGHER"
I know my answer
*I don't want to*
"SHOW THAT YOU CARE"
outside my mind
my hand
is reaching
farther up
I'm trying
I'm trying.

---

**President Decider**
By Harper and 3-306 Classmates

**Pressure**
You're the oldest.
Stop playing right now.
Do your challenge work.

**President Decider**
You don't always have to do your challenge work.
It's good for you to play, too.

**Worry**
What if we lose all our money?
You're spending too much money on books!

**President Decider**
Don't worry, you can always go to the library.
Those books don't cost any money.

*Harper and her classmates compose a collaborative poem featuring Harper's "President Decider," her wisest self.*

## Partnering With Families

Share these strategies with families for weaving the language into their home lives.

**Family members can incorporate this language in think-alouds.**

I've heard from families that weaving wisest-self language into think-alouds is a game changer. A casual think-aloud—during a moment when a parent is not reacting to a problem or explicitly trying to teach a lesson but just casually sharing a window into their inner dialogue—is an incredibly effective way to model how to listen to one's wisest self. Of course, it often doesn't feel effective in the moment. The parent shares, and the child doesn't even look up (or worse, looks up, blinks a few times as if to say, "You know, that did nothing for me," and then proceeds with whatever they were doing). Children simply haven't yet learned the disingenuous, if more socially acceptable, practice of feigning interest when someone shares something they aren't interested in. But they've heard their parent. And later, when they find themselves in a similar circumstance, they may try on wisest-self language, too.

**PARENT:** When I was a kid and it was time to go to camp, I'd feel this sort of achy-dread-y feeling mixed with a flippy-buzzy feeling. I'd think something along the lines of: *I definitely do not want to go.* And my wisest self would remind me it's okay to feel all sorts of conflicting feelings before doing a big new thing. The achiness and dread don't necessarily mean it's wrong to forge forward. It simply means a big change is coming! In the end, many of those camp experiences were full of adventure and joy.

**Families can use this language to help kids develop impulse control.**

**PARENT:** I understand that you want to snatch the toy out of your sister's hands. But when you feel the urge to snatch—and I feel it sometimes, too—remember that you don't *have* to listen to that part of you. You know a safer, more effective way to get it back. Listen to your wisest self that reminds you to use your words and ask her to hand it to you.

**Families can use this language to encourage kids to resist peer pressure.**

I recently heard clinical psychologist Becky Kennedy share an anecdote about how slow-to-warm kids (children who don't jump right into a new activity and who take time to observe before joining a group) are actually confident kids. Kennedy explains that these kids are listening to *themselves*, not to social pressure. Yet so often the language we use with those children ("I'm counting to five, and then you need to join. It's fine. Look, all your friends are doing it!") encourages them to ignore their instincts and instead to follow the herd. Fast-forward 10 years: The child is now a teenager who's been offered an illegal substance that everyone else is partaking in. If this teen's ability to listen to their wisest self has atrophied in the name of "following along" . . . you see where this is going. When kids don't jump in right away, instead of pushing them forward, Kennedy suggests saying, "You'll know when you're ready." In my view, that phrase is a lovely companion to wisest-self language.

**PARENT:** The choice is yours. Just listen to your wisest self. You'll know when you're ready to go down the water slide.

**Children and parents can brainstorm their own, family-specific language for their inner leaders and bring this language back into the classroom.**

**PARENT:** I think I'm going to call my inner leader my "true self." Because when I'm true to myself, I do what's right for me!

**EZRA:** I'm going to call it my "brain king." Because it gets to choose what to listen to and what to do. It's a really nice and smart king.

### BRAIN-CHANGING WORDS

## "Turn on your 'birder mindset': What will you notice?"

I often revisit (and repeat to myself) the advice that Marilynne Robinson's teacher, Ms. Soderling, gave her: "You will have to live with your mind every day of your life, so make sure you have a mind you want to live with." When attempting to follow that advice, cultivating emotional granularity and learning to listen to one's wisest self are only half of the equation.

If *we are what we pay attention to,* children also need to practice paying attention to tiny moments of joy, humor, or beauty that periodically emerge throughout their days at school (and beyond). Noticing these moments is an act of self-compassion because it makes kids' interior lives great company. Ordinary routines, such as walking down to the lunchroom, become more interesting. Many great philosophers across centuries and cultures have agreed: A key to happiness is the ability to find wonder in little things. Leo Tolstoy called these moments "gold in the sand"—jolts of joy that pierce the mundanity of being alive and make one's mind a lovely place to reside.

Before going to school, children are naturally great at finding "gold in the sand." A 4-year-old will spot a rock and shriek with joy because the stone fits so perfectly in the palm of her hand. A 2-year-old will crouch down and stare, hypnotized, at a luminescent beetle as it creeps along. Children are right to be bewitched by such things. It *is* extraordinary that we can touch a 400-million-year-old rock that may have been stepped on by a woolly mammoth and that we coexist with beetles that wear glow-in-the-dark body armor and survived the extinction event 65 million years ago.

But compliance-oriented school culture can drill this wonder out of kids. Children *already know* the secret to living a good life, yet we say nope, never mind, forget it. We tell them to stop dilly-dallying with bugs; to put away the rock; to sit quietly, memorize, and follow directions. In addition to snuffing out their natural capacity to look up and out and find joy, we've recently added a poison that social psychologist Johnathan Haidt (2024) calls "the great rewiring of childhood": social media that seizes kids' attention with unprecedented tenacity, bombarding them with images and comments that infect their mental health.

In this landscape, it feels more urgent than ever that teachers give children permission and space to reactivate the part of their brains that searches for, and pays attention to, small moments of delight. Here's where "birder mindset" language comes in: Birders find wonder and beauty in something that might seem mundane or unimportant. A birder sees a Yellow-bellied Sapsucker and stops in his tracks, transfixed. (This feels like an appropriate response to me: When did we collectively normalize birds, these flocks of tiny, flapping dinosaurs?)

When students internalize birder-mindset language and search for delight in ordinary moments, they notice things they'd otherwise miss. *They feel and do better at school.*

Walking to recess playing the "look and listen for an odd duck" game (instructions on page 78) makes the transition more engaging, so challenging behavior in the hallway decreases.

And about challenging behavior: A Brooklyn principal recently told me that engagement in elementary school classrooms has disintegrated and behavioral challenges have skyrocketed. This trend is directly connected to kids' atrophying attention spans. Children are so used to "novelty hits" through screen-based media that doing a non-preferred task (such as playing with blocks or completing a puzzle) simply doesn't hold their interest. "An emptiness comes from the combination of over-the-top unnatural sources of reward and the inevitability of habituation; this is because unnaturally strong explosions of synthetic experience and sensation and pleasure evoke unnaturally strong degrees of habituation" (Sapolsky, 2017). Predictably, grown-ups' attention spans are shrinking, too. Most of us can only focus on one computer tab or screen for 47 seconds before turning our attention elsewhere (Mark, 2023).

Elementary schoolers need practice "turning on" their birder mindset—approaching new activities and experiences with sustained attention and through the lens of "what funny/joyful/interesting thing will happen here?" And kids are especially primed to notice these moments when they know they'll have space to name out loud, to share with peers or teachers, what they discover.

Poet Mary Oliver, a birder and an expert at finding beauty everywhere, left these instructions for living a good life: "Go outside. Be astonished. Tell about it."

It's the telling about it that helps the astonishment stick. Shaping language about nearly missed flickers of delight not only motivates children to be on the lookout for these moments and boosts their attentional stamina, it also helps these joyful moments linger within kids' interior lives.

## Introducing This Language

I like to introduce birder-mindset language in the context of a writing exercise in which the children walk around the school looking for small moments that delight them. Older students can jot down their noticings on the template at right (attached to a clipboard), and younger kids can verbally contribute ideas that the teacher jots down. Looking at the world with a birder mindset inspires all sorts of ideas for writing across genres.

Try a version of this:

**MS. LILY:** Today, I'm going to share a secret about being alive with you: Often, we find what we look for. When a birder goes outside and thinks, "I hope I see a cool bird today," most of the time, the birder *does* spot a bird.

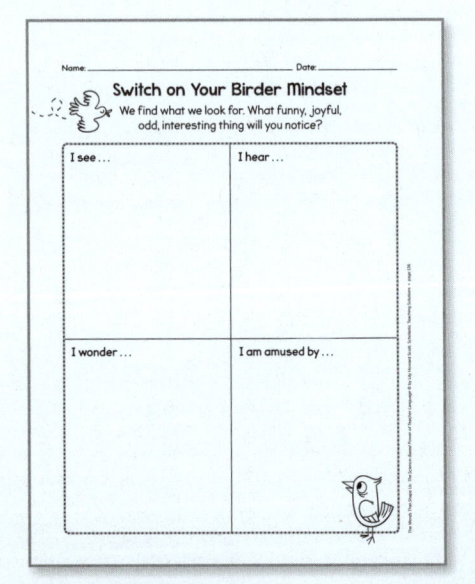

See page 136 for this reproducible template.

**MS. LILY:** Now, the bird might not be a Great Horned Owl; it might be an ordinary pigeon. But if you look closely at a pigeon, you'll find beauty. (Give me a mirror signal if you've ever noticed that shimmery, purply-blue-turquoise part of a pigeon's neck.) This year, when I say, "Turn on your birder mindset!," I don't mean to literally look for birds—though if you see one, great! I mean, *be on the lookout for a small thing that's beautiful, funny, or interesting to you*; something that delights you. Learning to move through the school day with a birder mindset not only helps us develop stronger, longer attention, it helps us enjoy learning more. Seeing like a birder, reading like a birder, listening like a birder—doing anything like a birder—makes our minds great company.

Here's how we're going to practice turning on our birder mindsets: Each of you will walk down the hallway, very quietly and attentively, with this recording sheet and a clipboard. You'll jot down what you notice. Then, let's see if those noticings inspire ideas for writing!

### Switch on your BIRDER MINDSET:
*We find what we look for: what funny, joyful, odd, interesting thing will you notice?*

| I see... | I hear... |
|---|---|
| • A Kindergartner on the rug pretending to be a snake | • "Bum bada bum bum!" |
| • A fifth grader reading to a first grader in the hallway – The first grader is taking off his shoes and they're both laughing | • A ukulele |
| | • "I was born to be Elsa!" |

| I wonder... | I am amused by... |
|---|---|
| • What if a Kindergartner pretended to be a snake *all* day long? | • The Fifth grader and the First grader being silly. |

**I'm a Snake Today**

There's not much I can do today
But slither and sort of sway

I can't put my backpack away
but I'll hiss at you, okay?

I can't hold a pencil, it's true
but I can squeeze you till you're blue

Sorry it's inconvenient
There's nothing to be done

(Though maybe you'll admit
This is actually pretty fun.)

(above left) Older kids can jot down their thoughts on this template.

(above right) The kindergartner slithering around like a snake (top left of recording sheet) inspired this poem.

(bottom right) Younger children can dictate their noticings to their teacher, who might paste them on chart paper.

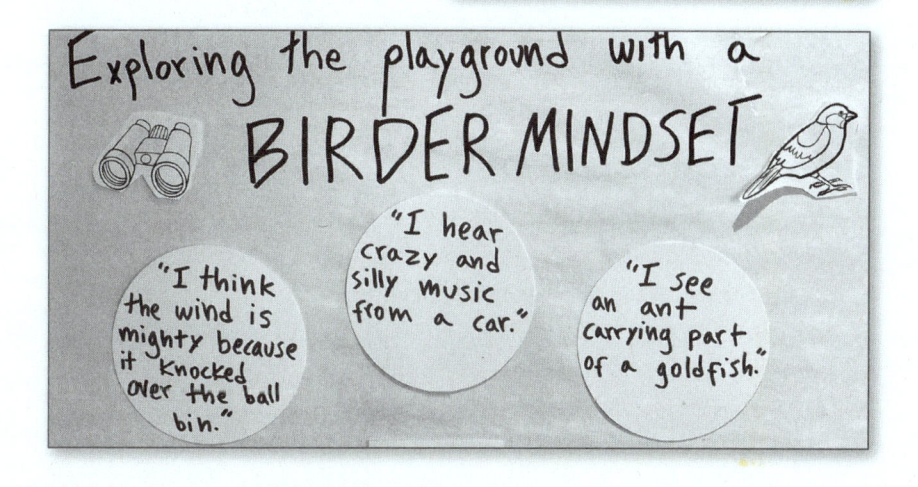

### Exploring the playground with a BIRDER MINDSET

"I think the wind is mighty because it knocked over the ball bin."

"I hear crazy and silly music from a car."

"I see an ant carrying part of a goldfish."

Part 2: Cultivate Students' Self-Awareness, Self-Compassion, and Self-Regulation

## Kids' Turn

Here are some ways children can use and internalize this language.

- In pairs, older students can "listen like a birder" as they take turns sharing funny stories. What specific phrases or anecdotes pop out to the listener? Invite partners to share this feedback with each other.

- Before exploring a new material—kinetic sand, pattern blocks, water beads—younger kids can turn on their birder mindsets and choose one secret special noticing to hold on to. (The excitement of "spying" for something interesting or surprising holds their attention throughout this exercise.) Once all children have given a thumbs-up indicating that they've tucked away their noticing, ring a chime and invite them to share these secret observations with a partner.

    **EMERY:** I noticed that the water beads feel so slippy and slidey, like someone painted jelly beans in magic slippery goo!

- In the context of the "look and listen for an odd duck" hallway or stairwell game, encourage children to silently tuck away one amusing thing they see or hear on their way to lunch or recess as they walk around the school. Then, when they reach their destination, they can share their noticing with a partner. (Kids delight in noticing the same thing.) This game keeps children attentive and searching for "gold in the sand" throughout an everyday routine.

    **POPPY:** On the first-grade bulletin board, I noticed a drawing of a kid riding a pig. I wonder if he *actually* rode a pig or if he just wishes he could?

- As a closing circle share, kids can share about small things that brought them delight or piqued their interest throughout the school day. Keeping an anchor chart like this one (below) visible helps kids remember to keep their birder mindsets switched on, and before long, it's permanently switched on. As Ross Gay (2019) writes, "The more you study delight, the more delight there is to study."

---

**Keep your birder mindset permanently turned ON:**

**Keep an eye out for:**
* Small things that make you smile or wonder
* Interesting things all around you
    * **Outside:** trees, sticks, rocks, flowers, stray garbage, anything at all. What delights you? What questions come to mind?
    * **Inside:** glue sticks, crackers, paint. How did these things come to be in this classroom, in your hand? Do you have any questions about how they were made?

**Keep an ear out for:**
* Music and rhythmic sounds all around you
* Interesting turns of phrase or playful language you overhear

**Keep a heart out for:**
* Micro-moments that move you: a moment in read-aloud, an interaction you witness, anything that makes your heart swell

# Curricular Connections

Apply the language across subject areas with these ideas.

### Take-Home Pocket Notebooks: What Will You Notice?

Kids of all ages love taking home these pocket-size notebooks. Simply sketch a bird on the cover (or have kids do this themselves) and write "What will you notice?" on the inside cover. (For a double-sided reproducible template, see pages 137–138.) Carrying around these tiny notebooks inspires children to pay attention to the world around them, and they can jot down or draw what they discover. The joy of these little notebooks is that kids have autonomy; they're "assignment-free." That said, many kids love bringing their pocket notebooks to and from school and sharing their noticings with peers and teachers. Inevitably, some of what children capture within these notebooks makes their way into their schoolwork.

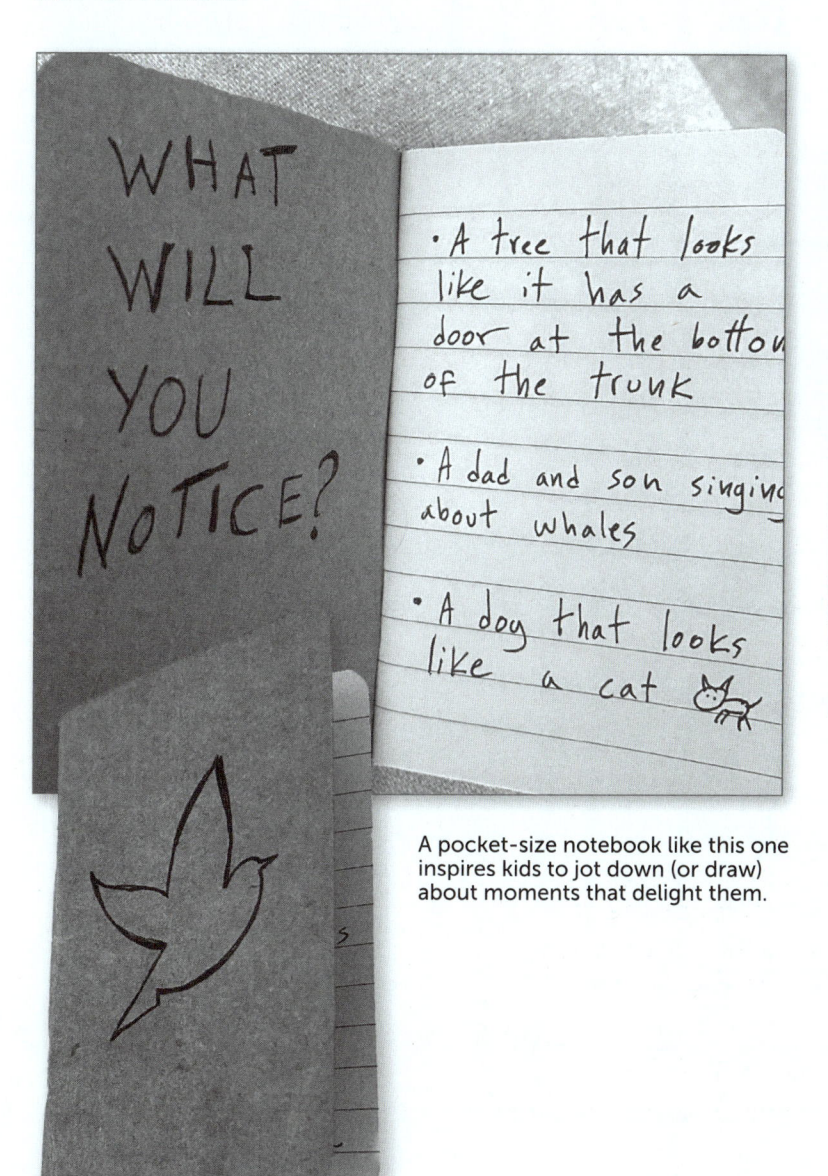

A pocket-size notebook like this one inspires kids to jot down (or draw) about moments that delight them.

See pages 137–138 for this reproducible template.

Part 2: Cultivate Students' Self-Awareness, Self-Compassion, and Self-Regulation

**Reading Response: Read Like a Birder: Celebrating Craft Jots**

Asking elementary school children to analyze author/illustrator craft is a tall order. But birder-mindset language encourages kids to keep an eye out for craft moves that delight them. Younger children can simply draw the bird symbol and verbally share their ideas with teachers or classmates, while older students can jot down their thinking underneath the symbols.

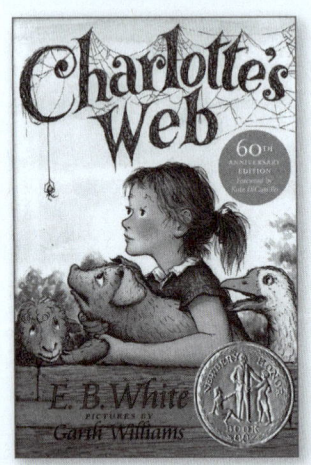

> Read like a birder
>
> Pay close attention: what elements of author or illustrator craft _delight_ you?
>
> • On your post-it / in your notebook, draw a ∨ and explain why.

> I ♡ THIS SENTENCE!!!
>
> "The barn... smelled of the perspiration of tired horses and the wonderful sweet breath of patient cows."

(right) On a sticky note, I model jotting down a sentence that delights me.

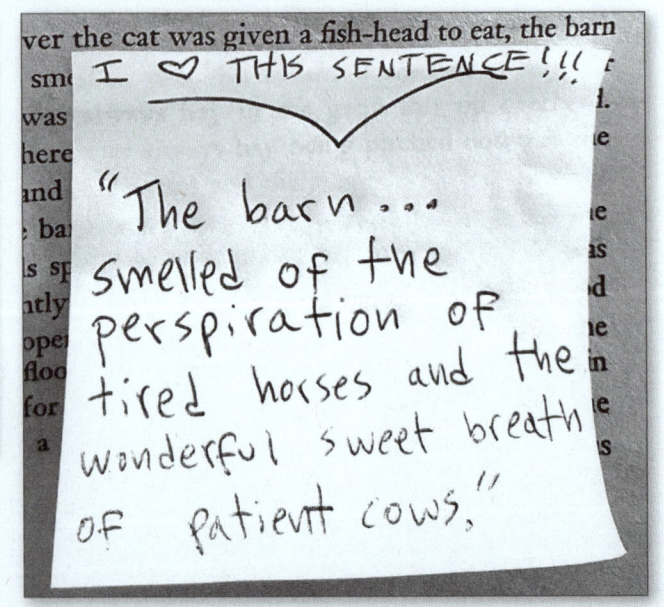

**Poetry Invitation: Birder Mindset**

When kids begin to move through their days with a birder mindset, they find flecks of beauty and interest and wonder—in other words, they find *poetry*—everywhere. Poet Max Ritvo (Ruhl & Ritvo, 2018) explains: "Learn to love everything and the world becomes heaven." Consider asking kids to write poems about the micro-moments of poetry they discover when they switch on their birder mindsets.

My former student Elijah, who always seemed to have his birder mindset on high alert, wrote the poem at right.

## Partnering With Families

Share these strategies with families for weaving the language into their home lives.

**Parents can use this language on run-of-the-mill outings with children.**

Parents report that the phrase "I'm bored!" is ever-present these days. (Maybe it always has been.) Approaching family activities and errands with a birder mindset inspires kids *and* parents to search for delight in everyday moments and lays the groundwork for connection.

Now, about connection: Elementary school–age kids want nothing more than to connect with their parents; to feel valued and heard. When a parent says something like, "Let's turn on our birder mindsets as we walk to the park. It's such a busy, beautiful day. I can't wait to hear what you notice!" and then attentively listens to whatever their child shares, the parent sends an important message: *I'm truly interested in your unique experience of the world.* The child's one-of-a-kind observations and insights matter to them.

> **Living Poetry**
> by Elijah
>
> Poetry
> is everywhere
> in everything
>
> Poetry
> is words,
> markers,
> the wall,
> anything!
>
> Imagine
> how the rug feels
> About being sat on.
> Write a poem about it.
>
> You can find poetry anywhere
> you look
>
> A speck of dust
> a subway conversation
> the neighborhood
>
> Don't hold onto your poetry
> let it run free
> just
> like
> you.

**GAEL:** I'm so bored.

**PARENT:** Let's look and listen like birders together as we wait in line to buy tickets. From now until we reach the front, let's see if we can each "catch" two things that are funny, beautiful, or strange. Go!

**GAEL:** I saw a dog jumping up, trying to lick the lollipop of a toddler in a stroller! And I heard a kid screaming, "I'M A SWAB KITTEN, NOT JOSHUA!" and I have no idea what a swab kitten is. But I wish I did!

## BRAIN-CHANGING WORDS
## *"I spotlight you!"*

This language is inspired by my former student Teddy. Teddy is a brilliant, always-true-to-himself child who, as a third grader, preferred reading novels to much else. (Sometimes, during math workshop, I'd catch him buried in a thick book hidden halfway under his desk.) At Teddy's fall parent-teacher conference, his mother Katie shared an anecdote that astounded my co-teacher Anneliese and me. Walking down the street, Teddy had noticed someone on a bicycle zooming by him. He turned to his mother and said, "To me, that person on the bicycle is just a dot, whooshing by me. But to that person, we're all dots whooshing past him. We all think we're the most important dot in the world, but everyone else thinks they're the most important dot in the world, and we're just a dot they passed."

Teddy's realization that each one of us is the center of our own universe, and that we move through the world with our own unique way of seeing things, demonstrated remarkable metacognition. I thought to myself: *Once again, I've underestimated what 8-year-olds can do.* I wondered how I could help Teddy and his classmates explore the gifts and limits of their own perspectives.

As children become comfortable thinking more metacognitively and deliberately—naming their feeling visitors, listening to their wisest selves, turning on their birder mindsets—they become ready for the next frontier of self-awareness: understanding where their perspective ends and someone else's begins. Infants believe they *are* their caregiver. Young children believe that because they love vanilla ice cream, others must, too. Older children believe if they think something is unfair, everyone else should agree. Indeed, many people never lose that way of thinking. We all know adults who regard their opinions as the only reasonable ones or who give advice that validates only their own experiences.

The spotlight metaphor, which has its roots in process-oriented creative drama practices, interrupts the inclination to assume that one's own perspective is ubiquitous. The language "I spotlight you!" inspires children to envision their one-of-a-kind perspectives as discreet circles of light that are *separate* from their classmates' circles of light. This language also sets the stage for empathy as children experiment with explicitly stepping outside of their own spotlights to imagine someone else's. During a read-aloud, a teacher might say, "I'm going to ask you to step *outside* of your spotlight, your unique way of moving through the world, and *into* the character Joe's spotlight. He has an auditory processing disorder, and he forgot his earplugs for the lunch room. As Joe, what might be going through your head?" Spotlighting invitations like this one encourage children to embrace what English professor Peter Elbow (2008) calls "the believing game": the willingness to explore and understand ideas and experiences very different from their own. (Elbow contrasts this approach with what he calls "the doubting game": skepticism that ideas and experiences very different from their own have legitimacy or value.)

Spotlighting especially comes in handy as children navigate conflict. A teacher might say, "First, I'm going to spotlight Naya. She's going to share her experience of the incident, which might be very different from your experience, Joshua. That's okay. Then I'll spotlight you." Spotlighting minimizes interruptions because it reinforces the idea that only *one* person is illuminated at a time and that whatever is shared within the spotlight is an impression or experience unique to the speaker and rarely universal truth.

## Introducing This Language

I love introducing spotlighting in the context of an interactive read-aloud. Whether you're reading a picture book to prekindergartners or a novel to fifth graders, you can pause briefly to spotlight any student by asking the child to imagine and inhibit the perspective of a certain character. With young children, you might walk around the rug area, tap a child on the shoulder, and say, "Turn on your imagination—I spotlight you!" to invite the child to embody a certain character with a facial expression. With older students, you can pause the read-aloud and say something like, "I spotlight you—what internal conflict are you wrestling with right now?" It's especially powerful to spotlight two characters on either side of a conflict. As kids become adept at imagining two very different experiences of the same moment in the context of literature, it's easier for them to lean into this duality in their own lives.

Below, I share how I introduce this language as I read aloud *The Case for Loving: The Fight for Interracial Marriage,* written by Selina Alko and illustrated by Sean Qualls. This picture book is about how Mildred and Richard Loving's advocacy led to the landmark *Loving v. Virginia* Supreme Court decision, which legalized interracial marriage across the United States. Alko and Qualls are themselves an interracial couple, and they shared that they were inspired to write this book because of the strong personal connection they felt—their "mirror"—to Richard and Mildred Loving's story.

Try a version of this:

**MS. LILY:** Today, as I read aloud *The Case for Loving: The Fight for Interracial Marriage,* we're going to do something new. We're going to use our imaginations to step *out* of our own perspectives and *into* the perspectives of the characters in this story through a practice called "spotlighting." When I spotlight you, I'm inviting you to imagine a character's inner life and to share ideas and answer questions *as if you were that character*. Now, I want to be clear about something: Of course we'll never know how Mildred and Richard Loving felt or what they were thinking as they fought to legalize interracial marriage. But that truth shouldn't stop us from being curious about, and imagining, their interior worlds. Imagination is a key to empathy, and only by empathizing with the perspectives of others can we become people who advocate for a kinder, fairer world.

**MS. LILY:** Let's stop on this page [see below]. After getting married in Washington, D.C., and heading back home to Virginia to live near their families, Mildred and Richard were told by the police that they needed to head back to Washington because interracial marriage was not yet legal in Virginia. As you can see here, Mildred is saying goodbye to her mother. What do you imagine she's thinking and feeling? Please turn on your imagination—click! When I tap you on the shoulder and say, "I spotlight you," you can share what you're thinking as Mildred. Put a thumb up if you're ready for a spotlight!

**CAMILA:** I can't believe I have to leave my mom. I could really use her help when the baby is born. What can't we all stay together? This is the most unfair thing in the world.

**MS. LILY:** Now, let's imagine Mildred's mother's perspective. Thumb up when you're ready!

**SYBIL:** It's just so sad. I can't believe she's going to Washington and starting a family. I guess Richard really means the world to her.

This student expanded on her spotlight insight (from Mildred's mother's perspective) through a "spotlight jot" reading response. See Curricular Connection, page 86.

The Words That Shape Us

# Kids' Turn

Here are some ways children can use and internalize this language.

- In the context of working together as a group, children can use spotlighting language to ensure all perspectives are heard and validated:

   **GAEL:** Okay, before we start gluing, let's each share which pictures we want on the poster board so we can make sure there's enough space for all of them. Emily, do you want the first spotlight? (And remember: No discussion until everyone's had a turn!)

- In the context of sharing math strategies:

   **MS. LILY:** There are so many wonderfully different ways you might solve this problem in your head. Once you have your answer, think carefully about how you'd put your strategy into words, and when I spotlight you, narrate your process. As you listen to your peers' strategies, get your silent window and mirror signals ready!

   **ISABELLA:** 32 + 49: I dealt with the tens first. I know 30 and 40 make 70. Then I turned to the ones, 2 and 9. I immediately saw another 10 in there and a leftover 1. So, 70 plus 10 is 80; 80 plus 1 is 81!

- In the context of resolving conflict independently, before asking for a teacher's support:

   **JADE:** Okay, let's try spotlighting because we keep talking over each other, and it's super frustrating. How about I go first, you go second. Want to try that?

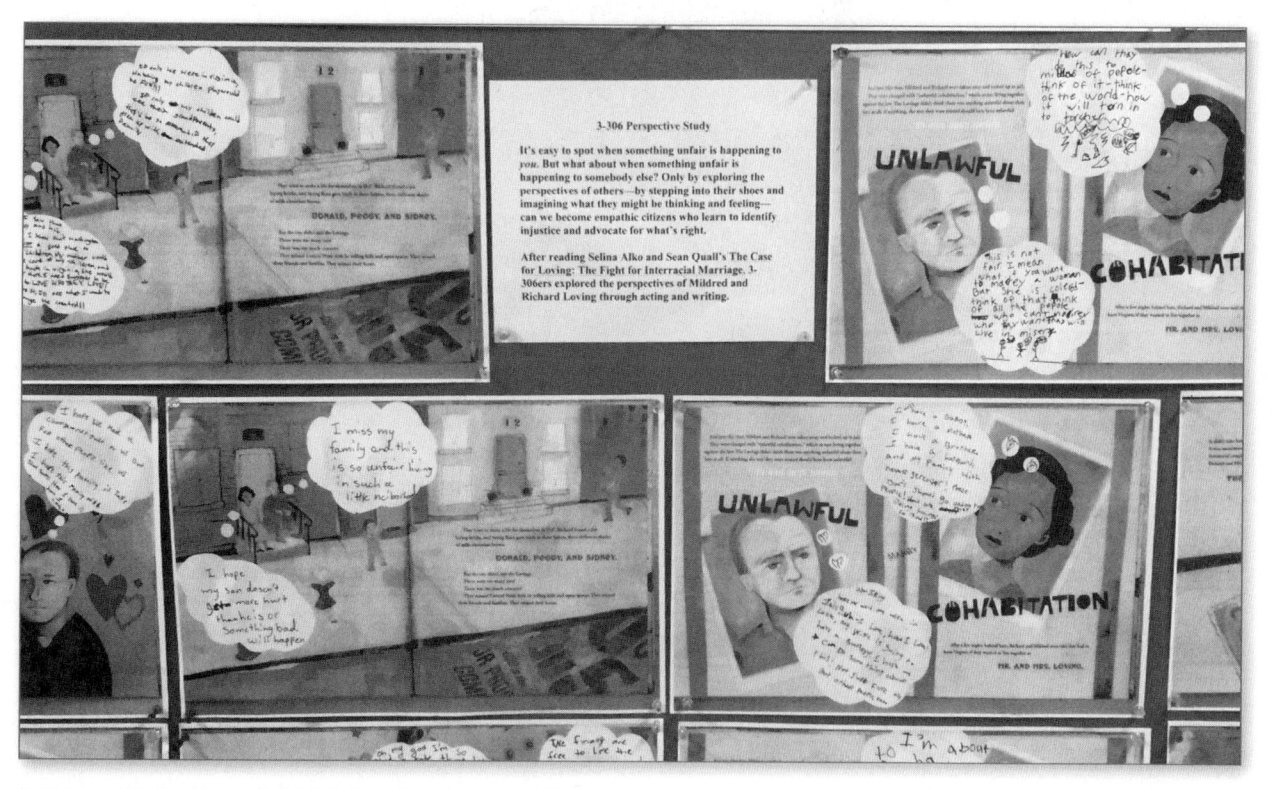

Bringing children's spotlight jots together is a reminder that no two children experience a book in the same way.

Part 2: Cultivate Students' Self-Awareness, Self-Compassion, and Self-Regulation

# Curricular Connection

Apply the language across subject areas with this idea.

**Reading Response: Spotlighting Picture Books and Photographs**

Spotlight jots are a creative, non-pressurized way to get kids writing about reading. For picture-book jots, simply tape a thought bubble onto an illustration, display the page underneath a document camera, and ask students to jot about what a character might be thinking or feeling. This exercise is an antidote to the one-size-fits-all approach to teaching reading comprehension that leads to high achievement on standardized tests and low engagement with actual books. Students' varied spotlight jots reinforce the truth that reading is a *personal* interaction between the reader and the text; no two children experience a book in the same way. (See bulletin-board display on page 85.) Kids bring their own background knowledge, mind movies, mirrors, windows, and so much more to every book they read.

Spotlight jots can easily be woven throughout social studies curricula. Below right, a student imagines the perspective of a Chinese American worker helping to build the transcontinental railroad.

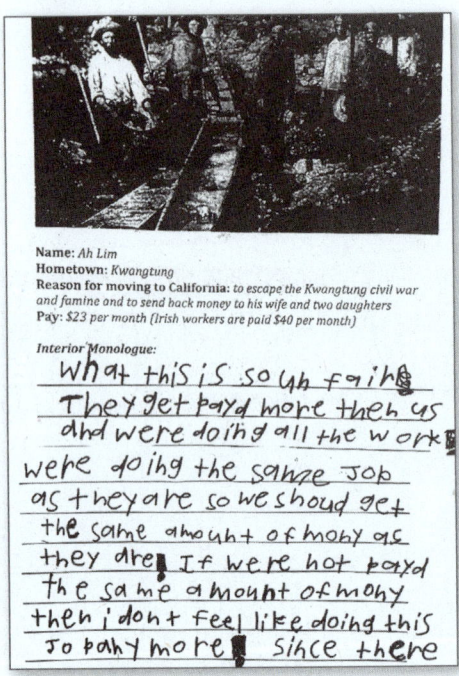

(above) A student imagines how a Chinese American working on the transcontinental railroad may have felt.

(left) Spotlighting characters' perspectives helps children cultivate empathy.

# Partnering With Families

Share this strategy with families for weaving the language into their home lives.

**Parents can use spotlighting language into discussions at home.**

Many teachers have had the amusing experience of telling parents about how wonderfully their child is doing at school (e.g., resilient throughout academic challenges; diplomatic in difficult social situations) only to have the parent say something like, "Really? At home, it's meltdown central." The good news is that unraveling at home is typical and healthy, a sign of a secure attachment. After holding things together in the classroom, many kids fall apart after school because they're back in their safe space, where they feel most unconditionally loved. The bad news (for parents!) is that there's typically a good deal more yelling and interrupting at home than at school, and many parents itch for language to help minimize siblings talking "at" each other and to help their kids navigate conflict in a more regulated way.

Spotlighting language can add a helpful structure to family discussions in which one sibling voice tends to dominate, and this language also empowers parents to remind children of my student Teddy's insight (see page 82): that their perspectives and experiences are unique to them.

**AALIYAH:** What she's saying is not true! What I did was *not* mean!

**PARENT:** I believe it didn't feel mean to you. But you're in your spotlight, and she's in hers. You two may have experienced the same moment very differently. Your choice may not have bothered you, but if she says it bothered her, it's important to acknowledge her perspective.

Spotlighting language reminds children that their perspectives *will* be heard.

Part 2: Cultivate Students' Self-Awareness, Self-Compassion, and Self-Regulation

# PART 3
# Inspire Students to Strive for Independence and Take Academic Risks

The focus of this section may be the most uncontroversial, universally sought-after goal of educators, regardless of their personal pedagogy. Every teacher hopes their students will learn to lean into academic challenges with independence, curiosity, and gusto.

But many of us go about achieving this goal in the wrong way. We dial up the pressure; we offer praise when students score highly; whether we mean to or not, we shame them when they don't. I've visited many schools where assessment scores are publicly posted on the walls and where educators tell children that mistakes are proof they aren't working hard enough.

> When we shame kids for not trying hard enough when they're trying with all their might, we teach them this toxic lesson: Trying doesn't work.

When I was teaching in Washington, D.C., a handwriting consultant held up a young child's work (ridden with backward *j*s, *p*s, and stray lines) and said, "The expectations of this worksheet couldn't have been clearer. So when you receive something like this, you know the student simply isn't trying hard enough." I stifled my desire to call out, "But how can you know that? Do we teachers have x-ray vision into kids' minds and experiences?" As I looked harder at the student's work, I noticed that the pencil lines were dark and deep, as if the child was pressing down with all her might, *trying*. In my experience, when it comes to handwriting, the work that looks absolutely perfect likely required the least effort because the child has already mastered the skill. Easy breezy, presto, done. It's the children who create letters that look labored and imperfect who are likely exhibiting the most effort. And when we shame kids for not trying hard enough when they're trying with all their might, we teach them this toxic lesson: Trying doesn't work. These kids—understandably—shy away from further challenges.

I recall a very different professional-development experience that, happily, inspired a joyful approach to navigating challenges. Cornelius Minor, then a literacy staff developer at Teachers' College, visited our classroom at P.S. 321. He explained that ==playfulness isn't "unsophisticated" or devoid of rigor; playfulness is all about attempting hard, even seemingly impossible things with a curious spirit.== It's about building a tower higher than you imagined you could, laughing when it falls down, and building it again with a stronger foundation. Minor encouraged our children to approach their literacy work with the same playful energy that they leaned into at recess. My students' eyes lit up, thrilled to see their own inherent capacity for playfulness as a strength, not a distraction, in the classroom. During Minor's lesson, which invited them to step outside of their comfort zones and attempt something brand-new, they embraced a "let's try that again!" ethos already so familiar to them from the playground.

Playful language—such as "What a brilliant mistake!," the snippet I shared in the introduction, or "Don't squish your ish!"—cultivates independence and joyful risk-taking. This section is all about the words kids can rely on to make "energized determinations" (Barrett, 2020) that encourage their brains to predict differently over time, empowering them to tackle academic challenges with resilience and joy, not avoidance or a cold sweat.

When children approach learning with playful energy, they're more likely to take academic risks and persevere through challenges.

Part 3: Inspire Students to Strive for Independence and Take Academic Risks

## BRAIN-CHANGING WORDS
## "What a brilliant mistake!"

Stanford psychologist Carol Dweck's (2007) groundbreaking research about the power of mindset has fortunately made its way into thousands of classrooms. In a nutshell: Individuals with a *growth mindset*, who believe their abilities can be improved, are far more likely to flourish than individuals with a *fixed mindset*, who believe their abilities are static.[5] Dweck's theory rests on the miracle of neuroplasticity, the brain's ability to form and reorganize neural networks. Operating with a growth mindset—regularly trying and sticking with new, difficult things—literally changes our brains. And a key component of embracing a growth mindset is centered around not only noticing, but also *revisiting* the inevitable mistakes that accompany doing something hard. When children spend time considering these mistakes and correlating "aha!" moments, their brains create neural pathways that enable them to retain new learning.

But who would want to linger on their past mistakes if doing so triggered a wave of embarrassment? Here's where "brilliant mistake" language comes in: This particular combination of words has liberated so many students from their sheepishness around making and investigating their errors. Many teachers normalize mistakes by modeling mistake-making themselves, but the language they use can undercut their good intentions. A teacher who self-deprecatingly says, "Whoops! There I go again, making another silly mistake!" inadvertently signals that there's a touch of ridiculousness to the error. But when educators label mistakes and accompanying epiphanies as "brilliant"— as grounds for celebration, not shame—children follow suit. Internalizing this language literally rewires how kids' brains respond to errors. Students learn to persevere through challenges with a capacity to withstand the discomfort of failure, which in turn leads to increased independence.

Brilliant-mistake language is a balm for kids who make mistakes all the time *and* for kids who rarely do. Dweck's research reveals that, often, children who have been praised for being naturally gifted are the ones most at risk for developing fixed mindsets. On the rare occasions these students make mistakes, the experience is especially uncomfortable for them because it threatens their sense of themselves as infallible, which is tethered to their sense of self-worth. Brilliant-mistake language, as well as language that celebrates "process over product" ("I notice you are really working hard on your cursive letters!") instead of "product over process" ("Excellent, flawless work writing your cursive letters!") helps high-achieving kids embrace a growth mindset.

Finally, because brilliant-mistake language dissolves shame associated with failure, children feel empowered to share their ideas frequently and open-heartedly. They begin to participate with the goal of making a contribution, not the delivery of a "good" product or the "right" answer. In *The Art of Possibility*, Rosamund Stone Zander and Benjamin Zander write:

> Unlike success and failure, contribution has no other side. It is not arrived at by comparison. All at once I found that the fearful question, "Is it enough?" and

---

[5] Dweck has acknowledged some limitations of early growth mindset studies, and her recent research (Yeager et al., 2019) reveals that context is tremendously important: Mindset interventions are most successful when teachers *and* peers support a growth mindset culture.

the even more fearful question, "Am I loved for who I am, or for what I have accomplished?" could both be replaced by the joyful question, "How will I be a contribution today?"

When children participate through a contribution lens, they don't stifle the part of themselves that says, *Just give it a shot*. They don't let a fear of failure inhibit the wonderful ideas *inside* them from making their way *outside* of them. When a student makes a mistake publicly, you might even reference Zander and Zander's contribution language and say something like, "Oh, a brilliant mistake! Thank you for that contribution. Let's investigate it together; there's important learning here."

## Introducing This Language

Even with the littlest learners, it's possible to root brilliant-mistake language in neuroplasticity. You can introduce this language in many different ways: as a morning-meeting discussion question, in the context of establishing a Brilliant Mistake Wall, or in the context of creating a class-wide book about learning from mistakes. This last approach, which I model below, is especially successful with younger students because it gives them something actionable that they can jump into right away.

Try a version of this:

**MS. LILY:** Please give me a mirror signal if you've made a mistake before. Me, too! I make mistakes every day. Now, I'd like to share something fascinating with you, something that scientists only recently discovered: When we make a mistake, and then we notice the mistake and think about what we learned, our brains change. They get stronger and smarter. From now on, we're going to call our mistakes "brilliant mistakes" because they're such an important part of brilliant thinking. We're going to slow down, pay attention to our mistakes, and celebrate the learning they lead us to.

Today, we're each going to create one page of a class book that celebrates our mistakes and brilliant learning. On one half of the page, you'll draw or write about a mistake you made. On the other half of the page, you'll draw or write about the learning that the mistake offered you.

Here's my example: While visiting a cat shelter, I offered a kitten a toy. But the kitten looked scared and ran away to the other side of the room. I felt worried and sad because I'd frightened it! I didn't just walk away and forget about that hard moment, though. I looked at the cat and considered what might have gone wrong. I noticed that the kitten was wearing a red collar, and that's when I discovered my mistake: I *forgot* that the collar colors have special meanings! Cats with green collars are ready for toys; cats with red collars need space. I thought about my mistake and whispered to myself, "Remember, only offer toys to green-collared cats!"

See page 139 for the reproducible template.

**MS. LILY:** What's a mistake you've learned from, inside or outside of school?

**CAMILA:** I once jumped a little when I was walking with my cereal bowl because the song we were listening to said, "Jump!" and the milk splashed all over me. I learned that when you love a song and feel jumpy, it's important to always walk carefully holding cereal.

**EMERY:** One time I was counting jelly beans, and I just looked at them and counted. But the number I got did not match the real number of jelly beans. And I figured out that I need to slow down and put my finger on each jelly bean when I count!

## Kids' Turn

Here are some ways children can use and internalize this language.

- In the context of a Spot the Brilliant Mistake! mathematics exercise: In pairs, have children hunt for brilliant mistakes that have been "planted" on sample problems and discuss the corresponding learning.

- When students peer-edit one another's writing, they can draw light bulbs next to brilliant mistakes.

- Establish a classroom Brilliant Mistakes Wall, like the one below, and invite children to jot (or draw) about their mistakes and corresponding learning on sticky notes, and then post these notes on the wall. During Friday's closing circle, those who added to the wall can discuss their contributions and discoveries.

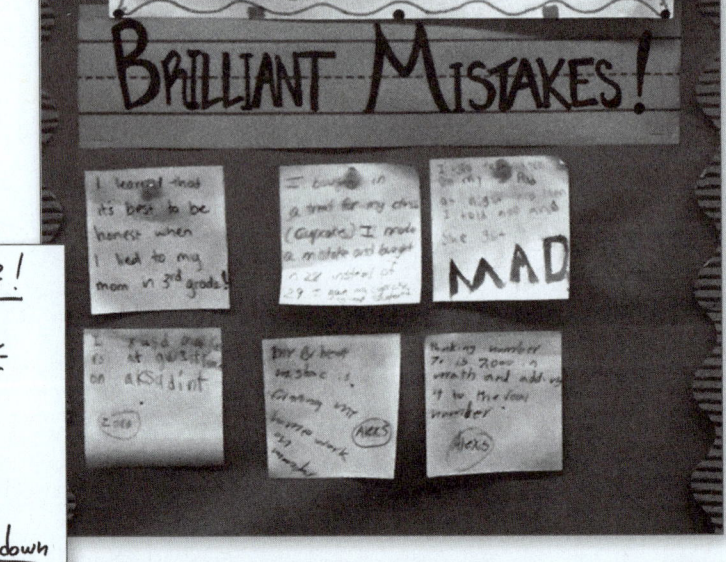

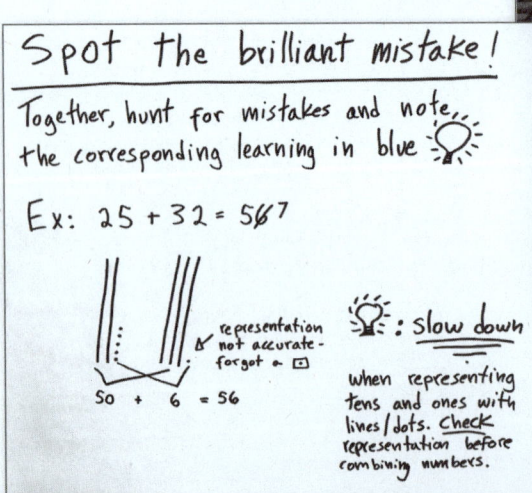

(left) Students can hunt for brilliant mistakes and associated learning in math problems.

(above) Invite students to post about their mistakes and epiphanies on the Brilliant Mistakes Wall.

- Incorporating children's suggestions, create a self-talk anchor chart to display in the classroom:

> **When you make a mistake, remind yourself:**
>
> * What can I learn here? Mistakes lead to learning only if I notice and explore them.
>
> * Some of the greatest discoveries of all time occurred because people were curious about their mistakes. (Chocolate chip cookies! Silly putty! Cheese!)
>
> * I can't control whether or not I make mistakes. (Even when I try my hardest not to make mistakes, I'll always make some.) But I *can* control how I respond to mistakes.

## Curricular Connection

Apply the language across subject areas with this idea.

### Collaborative Nonfiction Text: Brilliant Mistakes Throughout History

This is an older-student version of a collaborative text that celebrates mistakes. First, share the book *Mistakes That Worked*, by Charlotte Foltz Jones, with the class. Then invite each student to write about and illustrate a famous mistake and correlating invention featured in the book. (This doubles as an easy, low-stakes way to get to know your students as nonfiction writers before diving into a nonfiction writing unit.)

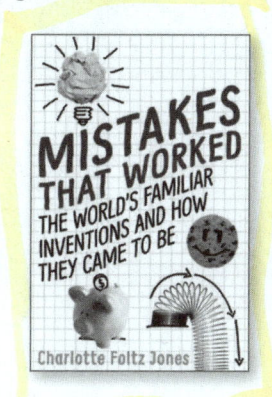

**MOLDY PETRI DISH -> PENICILLIN**

Dr. Alexander Fleming wasn't known for keeping his area of the lab clean. In fact, some people thought he was a pretty messy, careless scientist. In 1928, he came back to the lab from a two-week vacation and noticed some mold growing on a dish of bacteria he had left out. He *could* have thought: "Uh oh, my colleagues will think I'm really not on top of things, let me try to erase the evidence of my mistake." But no. That's not what he did. He looked carefully at the petri dish. He thought about the yucky mold, how it got there, and what it was doing. He noticed that the mold produced a self-defense chemical that killed some of the bacteria on the petri dish. By exploring his mistake, he made a world-altering discovery: penicillin.

Dr. Alexander Fleming has helped to save millions of lives because he wasn't too embarrassed to investigate his mistake. (And if you've ever taken that sort-of-gross, sort-of-good pink medicine because you have an ear infection, you can thank him, too.)

Alexander Fleming's mistake led to a brilliant discovery: penicillin.

## Partnering With Families

Share these strategies with families for weaving the language into their home lives.

**Kids can teach parents about the science behind investigating mistakes.**

I'm a fan of giving kids a night away from paper or computer-based homework and instead asking them to teach their parents about a specific idea we're exploring in class. (Children actually do this because they're thrilled not to have to do "real" homework, and parents appreciate a bit more insight into their child's school-day other than "good.") Consider asking kids to teach their parents about the concept of a brilliant mistake.

LUNA: Okay, my homework is to explain what a brilliant mistake is. It's a mistake you really pay attention to and learn from. Do you know when you don't feel too embarrassed by a mistake but instead you really think about it, your brain changes and you figure out things you wouldn't have if you *hadn't* made the mistake?

**Parents can share about their brilliant mistakes and correlating learning.**

Parents can swing by the classroom to share about their mistakes and accompanying epiphanies, and to take a few questions from students. They can also participate virtually or send along a brief video recording—whatever works!

Family members can share with each other about the brilliant learning hidden in mistakes.

## BRAIN-CHANGING WORDS

# "Let's approach our work today—and every day—with an 'ishful' spirit."

Perfectionist tendencies within young people are on the rise (Curran, 2023). There are a few possible culprits for this trend: increased parental involvement and supervision when it comes to monitoring grades and homework, increased pressure around standardized tests scores, and increased anxiety, generally. A culture of perfectionism is toxic for many reasons, one being that *perfectionism is the enemy of independence*. Teachers have seen for themselves how perfectionism manifests at school:

- Some children struggle to start assignments unless they feel absolutely sure about how to complete them "correctly."
- Others compulsively raise their hands and ask a teacher to check their work.
- Still others weep and crumple their papers when a creation doesn't conform precisely to their original intentions.

"Ishful" language injects a powerful dose of playfulness into classroom communities that tilt toward perfectionist habits. The term is inspired by Peter H. Reynolds's picture book *Ish*, a story about a little boy who tries to sketch various objects and, frustrated that his work doesn't look quite right, crumples up his drawings and throws them away. But his sister uncrumples his sketches and hangs them all up on a wall, explaining that even if the flower doesn't look exactly like the flower that her brother had in mind, it's "flower-ish." Approaching schoolwork with an ishful spirit and never "squishing your own ish" means getting started on an assignment even when you're unsure of exactly how to begin and remembering that what you end up drawing, writing, or creating will likely differ from what you originally imagined. In fact, what you bring forth may surprise you in all sorts of wonderful ways.

## Introducing This Language

After reading aloud *Ish* (which resonates with kids of all ages), ask children to take a stab at drawing something difficult with an "ishful" spirit.

Try a version of this:

**MS. LILY:** Today, I'm going to read aloud a book called *Ish*. This playful word has a lot to teach us about letting go of perfectionist tendencies and bravely trying new things.

Part 3: Inspire Students to Strive for Independence and Take Academic Risks

**MS. LILY:** Once Ramon, the main character, begins to think ishfully, the author writes that his sketches begin to "flow freely . . . quickly springing out, without worry." What a wonderful way to create and contribute—Ramon doesn't let self-consciousness or perfectionism stop him from getting started. Think of something you've always been interested in drawing but haven't attempted yet because the subject has felt too daunting, complicated, impossible. I know I've always wanted to draw an African elephant, but I stop myself before I get started. What comes to mind for you?

**THEO:** I've always wanted to draw space. But I don't even know how to *begin* drawing space!

**CORA:** I really wish I could draw a scorpion. Or a king cobra.

**MS. LILY:** Sometimes, we avoid creating something because we want to avoid the disappointment of watching the idea in our head come out differently, or worse, on the paper. But this avoidance prevents us from creating anything at all, which is too bad, because there is always beauty and surprise lurking in what we end up making. When we think ishfully, we get started and just see what happens.

Watch how I draw an African elephant on this piece of cardstock under the document camera. My marker is moving smoothly, freely, uninhibited. The tusks ended up longer than the trunk, and that's okay! In a minute, we're going to try something I call the "I Can Draw It-Ish!" challenge. I'm going to hand you cardstock squares, and I'd like you to ishfully sketch your tricky subject, completely independently.

Elephant-ish

Space-ish

# Kids' Turn

Here are some ways children can use and internalize this language.

- Kids can volunteer ideas for a "pledge-ish," a brilliant concept from digital learning specialist Anna Adam. A pledge-ish is a class agreement, like the one below, to embrace the values of ishfulness. Of course, this agreement will vary depending on students' age and the ideas they contribute. Kids can sign their names under the pledge (or if they are not yet writing their full names, they can write their first initials).

> **Our Pledge-ish**
>
> We pledge to hold onto our ishful spirits. We won't let perfectionism stop us from trying hard things, from letting our ideas breathe, from seeing where our pencils lead us. We won't squish our ish or anyone else's. We will look for beauty when what we create doesn't look exactly like we imagined it would.

- When kids overhear one another using self-defeating language, they can point to the pledge and remind one another to hold on to their ishful spirits. In our third-grade classroom, I heard children remind one another to "be ishful" multiple times per day.

**LYDIA:** Be ishful about it! You don't have to know exactly how to spell the word like it looks in books to just try to spell it. I'll still be able to read it.

Many years ago, a student created a funny little chicken and named it "the ishful chick," suggesting (to everyone's delight and immediate approval) that the chick be our class mascot. It lived in the front of the classroom all year long. Once, after a group of prospective parents visited my classroom during a particularly messy and collaborative art activity (read: total chaos), a child who noticed my moment of sheepishness walked up to me and said, "Art is ishful sometimes. Remember, don't be a perfectionist!"

- Co-create with children a list of self-talk prompts to display in the classroom, like the one below.

> **When I'm tempted to *squish my own ish*, I can...**
>
> * Remind myself that the greatest impediment to creativity is perfectionism.
> * Remember: First drafts, or first tries at anything, are usually messy.
> * Tell myself that ideas I haven't thought of yet will only come to me once I get started.
> * Remember: Nothing *anyone* creates turns out exactly like they imagined it would. But wonderful things lurk in the unexpected.

## Curricular Connection

Apply the language across subject areas with this idea.

### Free-Writes: Ishfully Dream Ideas Into Being

I love what writer and teacher Ralph Fletcher (2000) says about writing: "It's misleading to think of writers as special creatures. . . . Writers are ordinary people who like to write. They feel the urge to write, and they scratch that itch every chance they get." But so often, kids *don't* scratch that itch because they're self-conscious about "writing the right way." Ishfully Dream Ideas Into Being free-writes help children practice getting their ideas on paper in a low-stakes, joyful way.

Kids can take a stab at a free-write (like the one at right) for homework, as a morning do-now, or as an optional creative extension. Part of the charm of these free-writes is that they're completely separate from the curriculum and centered around silly themes.

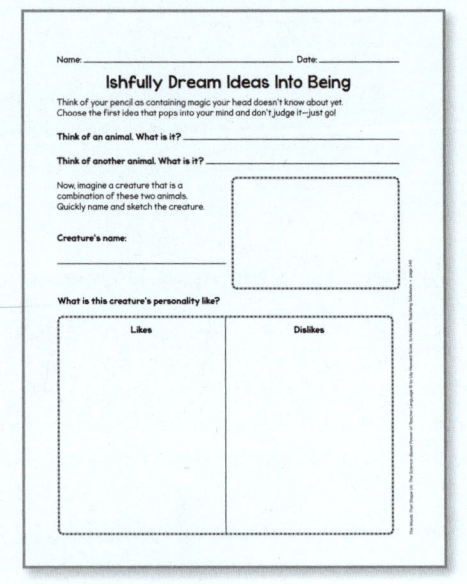

See page 140 for this reproducible template.

## Partnering With Families

Share these strategies with families for weaving the language into their home lives. When communicating with families about this language, it's important to emphasize that having an ishful spirit is not about doing something halfway or sloppily. It's about diving into challenging tasks with a spirit of playful independence.

### Parents can weave this language into think-alouds.

PARENT: I'm not *sure* how to draw a kangaroo, but that certainly won't stop me from trying! I'm going to draw a kangaroo-ish, letting my pencil lead the way.

### Parents can use this language when supporting kids with homework.

PARENT: I know you aren't sure how to begin your draft. But if I give you a lead for the introduction, the writing won't be yours. And what *you* bring to this draft is what will make it wonderful. As ideas come to you, try not to critique them too harshly—think ishfully and see what happens. You can always go back and revise later.

### Parents can share with the class about instances in which what they ended up creating was (happily!) different from what they intended to create.

Elementary schoolers can become very, very frustrated when what they create doesn't align with their initial vision. Parent sharers can help kids internalize the idea that nothing unfolds exactly as we imagine it will by sharing about moments when thinking ishfully helped them remain flexible and open to new possibilities.

## BRAIN-CHANGING WORDS

## *"Just take it bird by bird and do the next small right thing."*

Yes, I'm all about birds these days. But this second bird-centric language nugget serves a brand-new, essential goal: inspiring kids to break up challenges into manageable, non-panic-inducing bits. "Bird by bird" language comes from Anne Lamott (1995), a writer, teacher, and staunch opponent of perfectionism, which she describes as a habit that will "keep you cramped and insane your whole life." In Lamott's book *Bird by Bird* (1995), she writes:

> Thirty years ago my older brother, who was ten years old at the time, was trying to get a report written on birds that he'd had three months to write, which was due the next day. We were out at our family cabin in Bolinas, and he was at the kitchen table close to tears, surrounded by binder paper and pencils and unopened books about birds, immobilized by the hugeness of the task ahead. Then my father sat down beside him, put his arm around my brother's shoulder, and said, "Bird by bird, buddy. Just take it bird by bird."

Lamott's anecdote resonates with kids. They know how it feels to be overwhelmed by the vast scope of an endeavor in front of them, whether it's rebuilding a collapsed sandcastle or persevering through a complex mathematical word problem. Bird-by-bird language reminds children that all they have to do is tackle what's directly in front of them, do the next small right thing, and stop thinking so much about the goalpost in the distance. If ishful language helps kids get started on something that feels impossible, bird-by-bird language helps them keep going. It inspires children to break down complex-yet-concrete tasks into manageable bits and to navigate brand-new experiences full of unknowns. In both cases, the child simply has to proceed step by step, bird by bird.

Bird-by-bird language nestles within children's interior worlds and shows up in all sorts of contexts beyond school. When kids are learning a new board game, sport, or song, they can remind themselves that learning happens bird by bird; of course things won't "click" all at once. They simply need to keep doing the next small right thing, over and over again, until they get where they're going.

## Introducing This Language

You can introduce bird-by-bird language anytime—as a casual share, a morning-message discussion question, or alongside an especially complex, long-term academic endeavor, such as a nonfiction research project. However you choose to introduce the language, it's important to post the excerpt from *Bird by Bird* (above) somewhere in the classroom. Doing so not only attributes the language to Lamott but also succinctly explains the metaphor to substitute teachers, parents, and other visitors.

Try a version of this:

**MS. LILY:** Sometimes, when I'm tackling something I need to do—clean my home, finish writing a unit of study—the bigness of the task feels overwhelming. In these overwhelming moments, I rely on a snippet of language from one of my favorite authors, Anne Lamott: "bird by bird."

Let me explain what "bird by bird" means. Long ago, Lamott's brother waited until the very last minute to get started on a big school project about birds, which was due the next day. As he sat at the kitchen table, surrounded by unopened books about birds, he felt close to tears. How could he possibly get the report done? Lamott's dad sat down next to her brother and said, "Bird by bird, buddy. Just take it bird by bird."

Taking things bird by bird means doing the next small right thing over and over again, until you reach your goal. When you approach assignments, unknown experiences, *anything* bird by bird, you look just a few feet in front of you. Lamott compares this to a car's headlights moving through fog: You can see just a little bit ahead, and then before you know it, you're at your destination. When was an instance when you did something hard by going bird by bird, one small right thing at a time?

**LUNA:** When I learned to swim, I didn't put my face in the water for so long. Then one day I did. Then I learned to move my arms and legs at the same time and let the water sort of hold me. And then I swam!

## Kids' Turn

Here are some ways children can use and internalize this language.

- In the context of working together on a group project:

  **ROMAN:** Okay, let's bird-by-bird it. The next right thing is figuring out who will research which insect. If two people want the same one, we'll take it from there. Who wants the grasshopper?

- Older students can use bird-by-bird language when solving mathematical word problems and drafting fiction pieces, referencing these mirror anchor charts:

---

**Solving Word Problems, Bird by Bird: One small bit at a time**

* Read the problem **two times.**
* <u>Underline</u> the important words.
* Think: *What is the first step?*
* As you solve, write a little check next to the numbers you've already taken care of.
* Circle your answer.

---

**Drafting Your Fiction Pieces, Bird by Bird: One small bit at a time**

**Think:** *What small thing will I focus on now?*
Consider craft moves we've covered:
* Add sensory details
* Add inner thoughts
* Show-not-tell
* Keep the plot moving during an exciting moment
* Just let your pencil lead the way for one page and see what happens

**Do:** Whatever small thing you decide on, *do it*, don't question it. There is no wrong way to draft. You're off!

- Younger kids can reference this self-talk anchor chart below, using bird-by-bird language to help "slow down" the process of acknowledging and managing daily "feeling visitors." This language creates space between the emotional experience and the potentially explosive response.

> **Navigating Big Feelings Visitors, Bird by Bird**
>
> * Notice the physical sensation inside you.
>   *My stomach feels jumpy and hot.*
>
> * Name your feeling visitor.
>   *I feel angry.*
>
> * Listen to your wisest self and do the next small right thing.
>   *It's always okay to feel mad. Use your <u>words</u> to explain to a teacher or friend why you feel mad.*

## Curricular Connection

Apply the language across subject areas with this idea.

### Poetry Invitation: Break It Down, Bird by Bird

Invite children of all ages to write or dictate how-to poems, like the ones below, in which they break down tasks and routines (ordinary or abstract) into small, manageable bits.

---

How to tell the truth, bird by bird
By Lily

find it in your stomach
(if it makes you feel sick, maybe it wants to get out.)
give it a little attention

as the truth finds its way up into your throat
ask yourself:
does it feel like a tickle of relief?
or like luke-warm sadness
a hot water bottle
that's been lying around for too long?

either way—
think of who you want to tell it to
let the tickle or heaviness out.

---

How to put my brother to bed, bird by bird
By Alexander

make sure he didn't sneak something in his bed

sing the "robin hood and baby ruffie" song

if he wants you to change the words
then you sing the words that he changed

give him ten hugs

if he asks for more hugs,
give him more hugs.

## Partnering With Families

Share these strategies with families for weaving the language into their home lives.

**Parents can use this language to break down complex routines.**

When I was a new teacher, I once told a group of first graders, "Please pack up and come make a circle on the rug." A stampede ensued. Everyone crowded into the cubby area, backpacks flew, a few kids screamed. I said something like, "Wow, were my directions not clear?!" Of course they weren't. I hadn't modeled, or even mentioned, the steps of packing up in an orderly, calm way. What looked like "misbehavior" was simply confusion rooted in my own vague instructions.

At home, parents may sometimes assume that children already understand routines that are not yet fully clear to them. Bird-by-bird language can help parents break down routines into smaller steps, and when kids aren't successful, parents can more easily pinpoint where things went awry.

PARENT: I notice that things are getting hectic when we need to leave for school. Let's bird-by-bird it and draw pictures of all the next small right things we need to do before we go. We can tape these pictures to the door!

**Parents can use this language to help kids navigate challenging new experiences.**

JADE: At my old school, I knew where to sit at lunch and which part of the playground I liked and who my friends were. I don't know about anything now. I can't even picture this new school.

PARENT: Thank you so much for telling me. I completely understand why all these unknowns are hard. Here's the good news: *You don't need to know about everything at once.* Just go bird by bird and do the next small right thing over and over again. The first right thing is walking into your classroom and meeting your teacher, and I'll be right next to you for that part. The second is hugging me goodbye and joining the other kids. I'm not sure what the third next small right thing is, but *you* will know. Listen to yourself and go bird by bird every step of the way. You've got this.

Parents can use bird-by-bird language to help kids navigate challenges with increased confidence and self-reliance.

# PART 4

# Support Students When They Exhibit Challenging Behavior

When I first encountered clinical psychologist Ross Greene's theory (2014) about challenging behavior—"kids do well if they can"—I felt a wave of recognition. His words confirmed a truth that had been floating around inside me for years but remained just out of reach. The notion that children do well if they can may not bowl you over right away. As Greene explains, it only becomes an earth-shattering concept once you consider the alternative: "Kids do well if they want to."

The kids-do-well-if-they-want-to approach is popular and misguided. It's premised on the idea that when kids hit, scream, or refuse to do schoolwork, they must not be trying hard enough. And, the thought goes, we can remedy that lack of effort by offering rewards for behaviors we want to see and penalties for the ones we don't. Think sticker charts,[6] prize bins, demerits.

But, as Greene puts it, who doesn't want to do well? When kids exhibit challenging behavior, it's usually because *something is getting in their way*: They have a lagging skill, unmet need, or unsolved problem. If we want to help kids in their hardest moments, Greene advocates for a broader, more complex approach than simply incentivizing kids to modify their behavior. We need to identify the *root* of the behavior and empower students with specific coaching, strategies, and tools.

The wave of recognition I felt when I considered Greene's theory was tinged with sadness. I thought of my first year of teaching when I was committed to a kids-do-well-if-they-want-to mentality. Our school's administration had given each classroom a yardstick wrapped in different colored tape: green at the top, followed by yellow, orange, red, and at the very bottom, a foreboding blue square. I was instructed to clip 20 or so clothespins, each labeled with the name of one of our first-grade students, to the green top of the yardstick each morning. If a student "misbehaved"—talked out of turn, wiggled too much, exhibited other completely developmentally appropriate behavior—I was told to move the child's clip down the yardstick and to report the final color to the family at the end of the day. While I tried to avoid moving clips downward, I regret that I did not have the courage to refuse to use the system altogether.

---

[6] Some teachers have shared that in specific instances, a private sticker chart (that always leaves room to demonstrate improvement, no matter how much the child is struggling) can help cultivate self-awareness. Different things work for different kids. Private and positive, coupled with coaching and practice, may be helpful; public and punitive never is.

This approach to classroom management was counterproductive at best and deeply harmful at worst. The public embarrassment and stress that the young children in my care experienced as they watched the clip with their name on it—a physical representation of their identity—move downward to the "bad" color diminished their capacity to learn. Psychiatrist Bruce Perry (2021) explains: "The more threatened or stressed we are, the less access we have to the smart part of our brain, the cortex." The color-coded yardstick strategy also inhibited any learning associated with the moment of struggle: There was no discussion, no opportunity to practice a skill that could help the child do better next time; just an abstract, humiliating move to "yellow" or "orange." That school was full of excellent, caring educators and administrators who, to their credit, were willing to acknowledge and learn from their mistakes. Someone spoke up, and the administration has since revised their approach to classroom management.

For my part, I have embraced the polar-opposite approach to supporting students when they exhibit challenging behavior. This approach is rooted in Greene's kids-do-well-if-they-can ethos and the writer George Saunders's advice (Klein, 2021) about how to respond to others when they aren't behaving how we wish they would: "The only non-delusional response to the human condition is kindness." Saunders describes humans as "flawed thinking machines" who make endless incorrect assumptions about one another all day long. Years ago, I looked at a red-faced first grader who had just screamed, "I hate you! You're the worst teacher in the world!" and experienced a wave of humiliation: *He's trying to disrespect and embarrass me.* Now, with distance, I look at that moment and think, *Of course that wasn't what he was doing.* The child was struggling, defensive, reaching for words to bandage around something painful inside him and finding the wrong ones. As a flawed thinking machine myself, it really is delusional to believe that I can ever completely understand someone else's behavior and judge them as if I'm omniscient.

To be clear, I fail at withholding judgment all the time. And keeping Greene's and Saunders's words close doesn't mean I shouldn't erect boundaries, ensure that children understand and experience the consequences of their choices, or help them learn to repair. But it *does* mean that when things go off the rails—when kids hurl insults and hide in closets and pound the floor—I can try to see these behaviors in the most charitable light, not as personal affronts to my authority. Writer and teacher Don Miguel Ruiz (1997) advises: "Don't take anything personally." Easier said than done. But when we learn not to take our students' most extreme behaviors personally, we can respond to dysregulated students in a regulated state ourselves.

This section is all about language to rely on in our most difficult moments—moments when words usually fail us. When we feel attacked or stressed, we tend to say things we later regret. Indeed, it's a cruel trick that, in instances when our language matters the most, the right words are hardest to find. In an effort to make sense of something uncomfortable within us, we hastily shape words around turbulent emotional experiences and resort to language like the first grader used: "I hate you!", or, in a teacher's case: "Your constant chatter is *ruining* everyone's quiet time!" Words like these rarely reflect the truth. Is the student's whisper *really* ruining everyone's quiet time? Likely not. Tucking away the language suggestions in this section and sharing them with kids will help both you and your students get to a productive place faster. Most crucially, this language will help children navigate their hardest moments with dignity instead of shame, agency instead of hopelessness.

### BRAIN-CHANGING WORDS

## "You are always good inside even when you do not make a good choice."

Clinical psychologist Becky Kennedy (author of *Good Inside: A Guide to Becoming the Parent You Want to Be*) has popularized "good inside" language with parents around the world. This language is just as revelatory for teachers. Kennedy, like Greene, believes kids who exhibit challenging behavior are good kids having a hard time. And in those hard moments, the language we use to describe children can be self-fulfilling.

When we speak in broad strokes using language like, "You're rude!," we communicate to children that they *are* their negative choices. And if that is so, what is there to be done? How can kids possibly hope to make a better choice if they are intrinsically rude? Perhaps the most important thing we can impress upon our students is that they are still good people even when they do not make good choices. In challenging moments, vigilance about critiquing children's choices, rather than critiquing the children *themselves*, maintains their dignity and reminds them they always have the option to turn things around.

Imagine a kindergartner who elbows a classmate in line because she feels squished. You (the teacher) might say, "Hey, you're unsafe! Unacceptable. Please go to the end of the line immediately, and I don't want you to lay a finger on the classmate in front of you. Understood?" Or you might say, "You're always good inside, but that was not a good choice. Here are some words you can use to safely solve your problem: 'Can you please move forward?' Go ahead and give that a try now." This second option not only lets the child practice a new skill, but also reminds her that she is not her behavior.

Of course, when you say, "You're always good inside," the student may look at you like a deer in the headlights. Your words may seem to ricochet off her, just as "inner voice" language seemed to bounce off my son Alexander. But your words have entered her lexicon, and in a challenging moment later on, she'll revisit them. Perhaps she bops a classmate on the head with a recorder during music class, and her exasperated music teacher yells at her, and a feeling of self-loathing tells her she's "the bad kid." Another thought may swing by: *Well, my teacher did tell me I'm good inside even when I don't make good choices.*

This language is transformative for teachers, too, because it helps them look for the best in their students and see them with fresh eyes each day. It counteracts the powerful human inclination toward selective perception and anchoring bias, beautifully described by writer Angie Kim (2023) in *Happiness Falls*:

> There's a concept in heuristics called selective perception, a type of confirmation bias that describes the powerful human tendency to make assumptions and perceive things differently based on how they align with our expectations. You expect *x* to happen, something happens that's consistent with *x* (although also with *y* and *z*), so you decide *x* has happened. . . . Once you make that first assumption, another cognitive bias takes over: the anchoring bias, people's tendency to rely too heavily on the first piece of information we get on any given topic.

I've watched anchoring bias and selective perception sink their teeth into me throughout the school day. When I'm warned by other teachers about how difficult a student's behavior can be, I look for difficulty. When a child has an especially rough start to the day, I'm more on edge, more inclined to overreact or assume the worst in later moments. Reminding myself of children's inherent goodness helps me forgive what happened yesterday—or a few moments ago—and meet students with a hopeful, open mind.

## Introducing This Language

I like to introduce this language in the context of reading aloud Jory John's *The Bad Seed* (prekindergartners through fifth graders love this picture book) and a quick shared writing exercise, which generates student-created self-talk prompts. *The Bad Seed* also provides an opportunity for analyzing and critiquing author craft: How might students describe the seed differently than the author does?

Try a version of this:

**MS. LILY:** Everybody sitting on this rug—in fact, everybody in the world—struggles to make good choices sometimes. We do things we wish we hadn't, we say things we wish we didn't. When we make these choices, sometimes it can feel like we *are* bad. But here's the thing: Even when we make bad choices, we are always good inside.

Today, I'm going to read aloud a book called *The Bad Seed*. It's about a sunflower seed who learns that, even when he talks too loudly and cuts in line, his goodness never goes away. How do you think the seed felt when he overhears others calling him "bad"?

**CARTER:** It sort of seems like he felt he had to be "bad" because that's how everyone was talking about him. So, he was like, "Okay, I'll be bad."

**MS. LILY:** Right! The language we use to describe ourselves and each other really matters. And though the author doesn't explicitly say this, even when the seed made bad choices, he was never actually a "bad seed." He was always good inside. If the seed had overheard someone talking about him like this, it might have been easier for him to turn things around.

Think about a choice you've made that you're not proud of and tuck that choice within this phrase: "Even when I ____, I am still good inside." For example: "Even when I accidentally hurt someone's feelings, I am still good inside." When we remember our goodness, it's a whole lot easier to make good choices.

*Invite students to co-create an anchor chart by completing the phrase: "Even when I ____, I am good inside."*

# Kids' Turn

Here are some ways children can use and internalize this language.

- In the context of analyzing characters (see reading response extension in Curricular Connections below):

    **NORA:** In fairy tales or superhero stories, I've noticed there are pretty much just good guys and bad guys. In more complicated books, like *Crenshaw* (by Katherine Applegate), you can see that some people make terrible choices sometimes, but that doesn't necessarily mean they're terrible people.

- In the context of taking accountability for choices while also diplomatically standing up against negative, broad-stroke categorization:

    **EMERY:** Please stop calling me mean. I made a mean choice when I threw the water bottle. I'm really sorry about that.

# Curricular Connections

Apply the language across subject areas with these ideas.

## Reading Response: Beyond Traits

My colleague Gravity Goldberg recently pointed out that the term "character traits" is freighted with a whole lot of judgment. The term invites generalization: "That character is nice" or "That character is cruel." When children move away from this-character-*is*-this-or-*is*-that language and instead seek to understand a character's choices—"I wonder why this character is behaving cruelly?"—they become more sophisticated, probing readers. They also become more empathetic humans, moving away from black-and-white thinking and embracing this essential truth: No person is just one thing. Each of us is a jumble of all sorts of things, and a spark of goodness is usually in the mix, too.

The "Beyond Traits" reading response (right) is a foil to the character-trait web reading response with which so many elementary schoolers are already familiar. Not all the questions will resonate with students, so they can choose to respond to any four of the six questions.

See page 141 for this reproducible template.

For children who are too young to complete a reading response, simply moving from traits-oriented language to choice-oriented language encourages them to understand characters with more nuance.

### Teacher Resource: Keep-Your-Cool Strategies and Language for End-of-Rope Moments

An escalated grown-up can't soothe an escalated child. But it is *hard* to remain regulated when a child screams insults at you. The public nature of a classroom doesn't help: A child hurls a heavy book to the floor, yells something inappropriate, and looks right at you. Twenty-four of the child's peers turn to stare at you, too. What will you do? Teachers have shared with me that, in moments like these, they feel humiliated and overcome with the urge "to show everyone who's actually in charge." In challenging moments, I've felt incredulity and anger surge through me, too.

When it comes to projecting strength and steadiness, however, losing your cool simply doesn't work. If you yell, the dysregulated child may scream twice as loud. And even if the student immediately quiets down, they're not regulated; they're scared. The rest of the class is on edge, too, because the person in charge seems out of control. Responding to challenging moments in a calm, steady way does three things:

- It models regulation for the escalated student.
- It signals to everyone else that they have a reliable leader steering the ship.
- It ensures that you can look back at the interaction and feel peaceful about your response in the moment.

As teacher and psychologist Haim Ginott (1972) explains: "It is my response that decides whether a crisis will be escalated or de-escalated and a child humanized or dehumanized."

When we inevitably respond in ways we regret—as I have, many times—an authentic apology works wonders: "I was thinking about it, and I'm really sorry I yelled. I'm going to work on using a calmer tone next time." Becky Kennedy (2023) reminds us that repair prevents us from gaslighting kids: Our apology lets children know that they were *right* to think that something was "off" in how we spoke to them, and that they aren't to blame. We also model taking ownership for our own choices instead of implying that the child "made us" behave in a certain manner. By taking responsibility in this way—casually and without shame—we teach kids that they can do the same.

---

**Keep-Your-Cool Strategies and Language for End-of-Rope Moments**

**Strategies to keep your own sanity:**

- Picture the child's newborn-baby face in lieu of their real face. You are not in the midst of a power struggle between equals. *You already have the power.* You are the grown-up, you have the authority, you have nothing to "prove."
- Repeat Dr. Ross Greene's words to yourself: *Kids do well if they can. Something is getting in their way.*

**Things you might say to a highly escalated child:**

- **Create space between their wisest selves and their unsafe choices.**
  "No matter how hard of a day you're having, remember: You are not your unsafe choices. You are good and kind. And right now, you <u>can</u> make good, kind choices that will help you feel better."
- **Model a self-regulation technique.**
  "I'm going to stop talking and take four deep breaths."
- **Validate the child's perspective.**
  "I believe that this experience is really frustrating for you. Use your words to tell me how you feel instead of using your body. That way, I can better understand you and better help you."
- **Calmly set a boundary and give the child options.**
  "I won't let you continue hitting the bookshelf because it is not safe. Here are your choices: You can take your squeezie to the calm corner, or you can take a walk with _____. Which one do you choose?"

The Keep-Your-Cool strategies and language (sidebar, page 108) have helped me keep my cool throughout some of my hardest moments in the classroom. I hope you'll find them useful, too. Of course, sometimes—despite using your calmest, clearest language and relying on a wide variety of supportive strategies (more on these strategies in the next section)—the child in question will not calm down. Things might get worse before they get better. When this happens, be gentle on yourself. Despite the ostensibly supportive cultural narrative about teachers being superheroes, you do not have magic powers.

I recall one particularly hard morning a few years ago. A brilliant, sensitive child who was navigating significant emotional challenges needed to leave our classroom for a few hours. At lunchtime, the assistant principal walked into our classroom and found me in tears. I expressed my regret that I hadn't been able to support the child in the way I'd hoped to. She put her hand on my shoulder and said something I'll never forget: "Lily, you're not that powerful." Her words brought immediate relief: *Of course I'm not.* Once I released the pressure on myself to be a superhero, I didn't take this child's behavior as a reflection of my worth as a teacher. I collaborated with her parents and doctors openly and frequently. This child received the support she needed outside of school, and she found countless moments of joy and success in our classroom that year.

Writer Agnes Callard (2019) points out the high stakes of caring deeply for children: "The truth is, the story is not yet written, you care tremendously about how it goes and you don't get to write it. Which is all to say, the panic is justified." But letting go of the illusion of being a superhero—the illusion of control—helps us step outside of our internal "I must fix this!" frenzy and instead show up for our students with more resilience, presence, and support.

## Partnering With Families

Share these strategies with families for weaving the language into their home lives.

### Families can weave this language into read-aloud discussions.

For many children, it's easier to move away from essentializing another person as "bad" in the context of discussing a character. I recently introduced Ludwig Bemelmans's *Madeline* to my children. When we reached the page that reads, "They smiled at the good, and frowned at the bad," my 2-year-old son Charlie pointed to the illustration of someone sneaking away with a purse full of jewels and chirped, "Who's dat?" "A robber," I replied. My older son, Alexander, corrected me: "Mommy, you should say a person who is stealing, not 'a robber' because people aren't just *one thing*. Maybe he does good stuff, too." An excellent reminder, and a truth I hope he remembers during his next moment of conflict on the playground when he's tempted to call a classmate "a meanie."

This language around separating negative choices from one's inherent worth or goodness also invites children to analyze author language with a careful, critical eye. A few weeks after the *Madeline* read-aloud, I sang "What's the Use of Wond'rin'" from the musical *Carousel* as a bedtime lullaby. Alexander suggested I change the lyric "bad" to "bad choices": "What's the use of wond'rin' if he's good or if he just makes bad choices sometimes?" I made the requested adjustment. He paused and said, "Well, it does *sound* better the first way." (Rodgers and Hammerstein would agree, I think.) But this practice of not simply taking a description of someone else at face value—of considering how he might modify the language to make the characterization more specific, less judgmental—is one I hope he maintains and shares with others as he gets older.

ELOISE: That character is so mean.

PARENT: I also notice that this character is making all sorts of mean choices, like telling the other kids they're reading baby books. I wonder why she's doing that. Let's see what we can find out.

**Parents can use this language to remind children of their inherent goodness in a challenging moment.**

PARENT: You are so kind inside, and I've seen you share kindly many times before. Please go give the binoculars back to the child they belong to.

**Family members can offer up their own language adaptations for the idea of inherent goodness.**

A school leader who practices Quakerism calls this inherent goodness an "inner light." I know a parent who tells her daughter every evening, "Your heart is always good." Parents and children can offer up their own words, in any language, to capture this idea of inner decency and kindness.

The way adults speak to children becomes the way children speak to themselves. When parents remind kids of their inherent goodness, kids internalize this language.

### 💬 BRAIN-CHANGING WORDS

## "Different things are hard for different people. What about ___ feels hard for you/me?"

Say a first grader puts his head down on the desk and refuses to write a word. As a new teacher, I might have said something like, "Up, up, up you go! I believe in you!" But a well-intentioned phrase like this doesn't always feel so supportive to the child and can even imply that there's a hint of absurdity to his standstill. Back to Greene's thesis: *Kids do well if they can.* If that child isn't doing well, something is likely *hard* for him about meeting the expectations of the moment. Asking children to share what feels specifically hard for them about a task or expectation opens the door to actually solving the problem behind the behavior. Most importantly, asking this question honors students' perspectives and contributions: They possess valuable information that we don't, so let's listen to what they have to say.

Back to the child with his head down—saying a version of this can unlock solutions: "I notice that getting started with your writing seems hard for you right now. I have a mirror to this—I also struggle to get started sometimes. I'd love to know more about what feels *specifically* hard in this moment so we can brainstorm solutions." The student could say anything. Perhaps that morning, his older sister told him he's a bad writer; perhaps he can't think of any ideas; perhaps he's unsure about how to form a particular letter. Each of these answers would elicit different support strategies from you, and this child-centric, individualized coaching would likely trigger far more success than a blanket "I believe in you!" statement. Of course, you believe in the child; you're showing him you do by taking his input seriously.

One reason why teachers avoid asking kids about what's hard for them is because they might reasonably worry that such language will come across as sarcastic or patronizing: "I mean, really, what is so hard about that?" But we need to give ourselves more credit. Although there is much beyond our control when it comes to students' individual choices, we have tremendous influence in our ability to cultivate classroom cultures of warmth and vulnerability (or shame and fear). When we openly and appropriately share about our *own* areas for growth, kids follow our lead. And just as naming feelings creates distance between the child's identity and the feeling—I *have* the feeling, but I *am not* the feeling—naming these "hard things" creates space between the child's identity and the particular struggle. This space provides relief and reminds children that the hard thing is not who they are.

> **If that child isn't doing well, something is likely *hard* for him about meeting the expectations of the moment.**

Once my third-grade students became comfortable with the notion that different things are hard for different people, and honestly answered my question "What about ___ feels hard for you?," certain instances of challenging behavior evaporated. This is because I could finally provide appropriate coaching and strategies instead of simply attempting to modify behavior. I recall one student, Riley, who struggled with impulse control and repeatedly called out his ideas during read-alouds. Redirecting him, asking him to take a break, trying to think of a logical consequence for the constant call-outs—none of these

Part 4: Support Students When They Exhibit Challenging Behavior strategies worked. Finally, one day, I asked Riley to tell me what felt specifically hard for him about not calling out. Riley said, "I just have so many ideas in my head at once, and I'm worried if I don't say them right away, I'll forget them."

Now I had the information I needed to actually help him. I gave Riley a pencil and a clipboard covered with six sticky notes. We agreed that I'd call on him twice during the read-aloud to share his ideas, and after that he'd jot down his thoughts on the sticky notes, which he would read aloud to me during choice time later in the day. During that afternoon's read-aloud, Riley—his clipboard and sticky notes perched on his knees—did not call out once. Over time, he moved away from jotting on physical sticky notes to thinking of his ideas as "sticky notes in my head." And while Riley couldn't remember all of his mental notes (and he certainly still called out from time to time), imagining his thoughts as colorful squares that he tucked away within himself was the strategy he'd been missing, the tool that empowered him to make better choices.

> **FAIR ≠ EQUAL**
> Fair is getting what you need to be successful. And different kids need different things!
> ⇓
> Seating options! glasses! rug tools! Variations of assignments! different templates!

Incorporating students' suggestions, jot down examples of different tools they might notice around them.

I understand reticence around giving certain students enticing tools (e.g., a clipboard with sticky notes, extra wiggle breaks in the hallways, a certain pencil grip, or a weighted snake for rug time). Won't everyone else want the tool, too? Once again, the magic of a preview saves the day. Remind kids that *fair is not equal; fair is getting what you need to be successful*. In your classroom, different students will use different tools because they have different needs.

Naming this truth defuses the element of surprise and zaps outcries of injustice when a peer is handed a tool. Often, what alarms children is not the thing itself, but the *unexpectedness* of the thing or the confusion surrounding it. As Brené Brown (2018) teaches us: "Clear is kind. Unclear is unkind." Being crystal-clear about the reasoning and protocols around tool-use helps children know exactly what to expect, which in turn helps them remain regulated.

Sometimes, after a child has identified what's hard and is relying on specific strategies and tools to do better, the hard thing remains hard. The student might say something like, "I just can't do this." A phrase you can tuck away for moments like this is, "You are already doing this. The tremendous effort I see right now is you doing this, getting closer and closer to your goal." I learned of this language from Lauren Feit, an obstetrician. In the midst of a difficult labor, a patient of hers declared that she simply couldn't do it. Dr. Feit calmly countered, "You are already doing it." And on the hardest school day, when everything is going wrong and you feel like *you* can't do it (what teacher hasn't felt this way?!), Dr. Feit's language may be a comfort: *You are already doing it, minute by minute, bird by bird.*

# Introducing This Language

I like to introduce this language in the context of a brief class discussion about how different things are hard for different people. When sharing what's hard for me, I keep writer and educator Parker Palmer's words close (2007): "Face to face with my students, the only resource at my immediate command: my identity, my selfhood . . . am I willing to make it available and vulnerable in the service of learning?"

Try a version of this:

**MS. LILY:** Everybody in the entire world has "hard things." But it's easy to forget this. When I'm having a hard time with something, and I look at someone next to me who isn't having a hard time with that thing, I might tell myself, "Oh, everything must be easy for them." But that's simply not true: Something *else* is hard for that person; I just don't know what it is. Remembering that *different things are hard for different people* makes it easier to look within ourselves and identify—without shame!—what's hard for us. Once we've done that, we can think of strategies that can help us do better.

For example, something that's hard for me is keeping track of where I put my conferring clipboard. I'll put it down, and then, poof, one minute later, I have no idea where it is. You've all seen me looking high and low for it! Who has an idea for a strategy I can use to keep better track of where I put that clipboard?

**JONESE:** You could maybe have a special spot for it, like a hook on the wall with a yellow square made of painter's tape around it and a big sign that says PUT CLIPBOARD DOWN HERE instead of just hoping you'll remember where you leave it but never actually remembering.

**MS. LILY:** Wonderful suggestion! Thank you. Another hard thing for me is changing the plan. If I think one thing is going to happen, and then another thing happens, I can struggle to remain flexible. When a plan changes, a strategy I now rely on is saying to myself: *Go with the flow! Changing the plan can lead to good stuff you don't know about yet!"*

Today, with your help, we're going to make a list of some "hard things" we're navigating in this classroom. Throughout the year, we'll brainstorm strategies to help these hard things feel a bit easier.

What is something that can be hard for you? If a friend shares an idea you were going to contribute, be sure to give a mirror symbol.

**GAEL:** Waiting in line!

**CARTER:** Not starting at the reading center I want to start at.

**AALIYAH:** Getting calm when I feel so mad.

**LUNA:** Doing stuff I just really don't feel like doing.

**FRANCIS:** Stopping recess. I never, ever want to do that.

## Kids' Turn

Here are some ways children can use and internalize this language.

- In the context of a shared writing exercise, younger children can turn and talk to brainstorm strategies for managing these "hard things" and offer their contributions, which the teacher writes down in a projected document (like the one below) or on an anchor chart. Older students can independently complete the left-hand column of the chart, then partner up to brainstorm strategies.

**Different Things Are Hard for Different People**

Together, we can brainstorm strategies and tools!

| Things That Are Sometimes Hard for Me | Strategy Ideas |
|---|---|
| "Staying quiet in line when I really want to joke around with a friend." | "Always have your birder mindset on even when the teacher doesn't ask you to turn it on." |
| "Waiting for the swings when they're taken." | "Stay near the swing, but don't just wait. Play a game or sing a song to keep yourself busy and not so annoyed." |

- In the context of working together as a group, students can share about things that are hard for them (so their peers better understand how they work and why they're relying on certain tools):

**SEBASTIAN:** Something that can be hard for me is keeping my research organized. I'm going to jot down facts on these notecards Ms. M gave me instead of using the graphic organizers you have.

- In the context of sharing drafts with peer editors, older students can preview what they'd like them to look for:

**POPPY:** Something that can be hard for me is remembering the homonym rules. Will you keep an eye out for *there/their/they're* mix-ups as you read?

- In the context of sharing about their interior lives or resolving conflicts, children can use this language to explain the hard thing that lies beneath some of their challenging behavior:

  **CARLOS:** I'm sorry I ignored you both. I guess something that's hard for me is being okay with you having other best friends, too. I'm worried you'll end up liking them better.

- Kids can reference this self-talk anchor chart below.

> **When you're having a really hard time, remember:**
>
> Different things are hard for different people.
>
> **Ask yourself:** What feels hardest about this moment?
> * Is there a hope I have that isn't coming true?
> * Is there an expectation I have that isn't being met?
> * Is there a certain skill I'm having trouble mastering?
>
> Share your answers to these questions with a teacher so you can receive the support you need to do your best!

## Curricular Connection

Apply the language across subject areas with this idea.

### Reading Response: Beneath Behavior: What's Hard for ___?

As either a shared-writing reading response (younger kids) or an independent reading response (older students), children can explore how characters' "hard things" motivate certain behaviors.

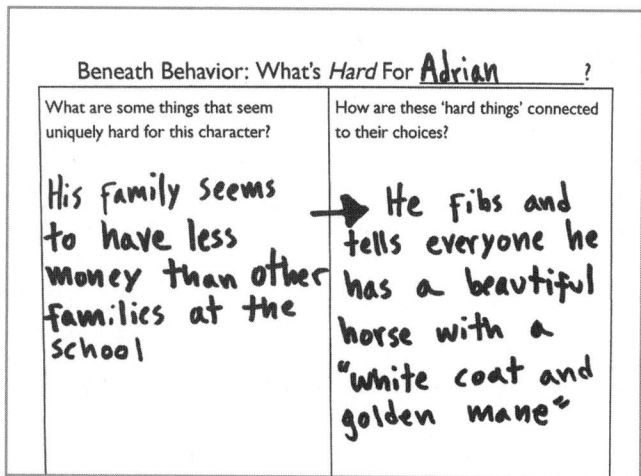

Beneath Behavior: What's *Hard* For **Adrian**?

| What are some things that seem uniquely hard for this character? | How are these 'hard things' connected to their choices? |
|---|---|
| His family seems to have less money than other families at the school | He fibs and tells everyone he has a beautiful horse with a "white coat and golden mane" |

See page 142 for a reproducible template.

Part 4: Support Students When They Exhibit Challenging Behavior

## Partnering With Families

Share these strategies with families for weaving the language into their home lives.

**Family members can use this language to uncover what's really going on in challenging moments.**

Greene's kids-do-well-if-they-can philosophy is a gift to parents. Once parents understand that their children's challenging behavior is often rooted in a lack of skill, not will, they can uncover solutions.

PARENT: I notice that when I ask you to clean up your room, you put a few things away and then stop. I understand that when it gets super messy, it's a big job. When you start cleaning, what specifically feels hard about keeping going?

CHILD: I put things away but it seems like nothing actually gets cleaner. No matter what, it's just hopeless. So I give up.

PARENT: What if we create a chart so you can keep track of your progress and more clearly "see" what you're accomplishing? You can check things off as you go!

**Parents can use this language as they think aloud about some things that are hard for them and model how to rely on certain strategies.**

PARENT: Something that can be hard for me is being in places that are loud and busy. I know this about myself. So sometimes when I'm in a hectic place, like an airport gate, here's what I do: I stand just a little bit away from the crowd and take a few moments of quiet in a calmer area. I make sure I can still see the gate, but I'm not right next to it. And I head back to where I need to be once it's time to board!

### BRAIN-CHANGING WORDS

# "Both/And"
# "Intent/Impact"

The ability to hold onto multiple, contradictory truths is essential to navigating challenges—or navigating anything, really—with diplomacy and nuance. But this skill doesn't come naturally. Our minds are wired to categorize, and we often take this tendency too far: *I'm a math person or I'm not; he's arrogant or he isn't.* "Either/or" thinking drives us to oversimplify things and embrace only one perspective or stance as legitimate. This is a problem because to be alive is to be surrounded by complex, conflicting truths. And if we refuse to acknowledge this multiplicity of truth, we won't see the world, each other, or ourselves clearly.

In *Both/And Thinking: Embracing Creative Tensions to Solve Your Toughest Problems*, Wendy K. Smith and Marianne W. Lewis (2022) define *paradox* as "contradictory, yet interdependent elements that exist simultaneously and persist over time." When we give children words (such as "both/and" and "intent/impact") to describe the paradoxes all around them, we empower them to move away from black-and-white thinking and toward a more openhearted, productive way of operating. When their assumptions are challenged, instead of thinking, "That can't be so, because I know ___ to be true," they instead think, "I wonder if ___ could be true *as well*?"

A few years ago, I used both/and language to explain differentiated seating to my students: "It is both true that you may do your best listening on the rug and that another student may do their best listening in a way that looks very different—perhaps from their desk, on a wiggle stool, or while sketching in a notepad." This both/and statement resonated with the children. In our ICT classroom, under the guidance of an excellent special educator (my co-teacher, Anneliese), our students understood that different kids learn in different ways. I learned from Anneliese that this core practice of special education—tailoring curricula and norms to children's strengths and needs instead of adhering to a one-size-fits-all set of expectations—is simply a tenet of *good* education. All students benefit from a differentiated, flexible, asset-based approach to learning.

A few months after this classroom conversation about differentiated seating, Anneliese and I left the students with a substitute teacher so we could attend a professional-development workshop during school hours. When we returned to the classroom, we found Nina (a slow-to-warm, deeply creative, neuroatypical child) crying in the corner, hugging her knees. A few children were comforting her, and the rest were emphatically trying to explain something to the substitute teacher. Apparently, the teacher had yelled at Nina when she refused to come sit on the rug with the other children. The children rallied to Nina's defense, saying things like, "But it's *okay* if she doesn't always come to the rug. Sometimes she sits at her desk!"

The substitute teacher had been leaning into an either/or mindset: Either you're listening in a way that looks like listening to me or you're not listening. The children had grasped a complexity that hadn't dawned on him: Different students listen in different ways. Anneliese and I beamed with pride at our students' advocacy on behalf of their classmate.

At its worst, either/or thinking can lead to a negative feedback loop that psychotherapist Esther Perel calls "splitting the ambivalence"—perceiving someone as having an unreasonable position ("That kid thinks he can get away with anything . . .") and compensating by retreating to the opposite pole and taking a more extreme stance than we otherwise would (". . . so I'll never, ever give an inch!"). Splitting the ambivalence snuffs out understanding and nuance, driving us into polarized stances. By contrast, embracing paradox triggers learning and forward momentum: "It is both true that I am a great mathematician and that I am feeling stuck, so I'm just going to skip this question and keep going." Or, "My intent was just to share my ideas, but my impact was that you didn't have time to share yours. I'm sorry—next time, you can go first."

The Nobel Prize-winning physicist Niels Bohr, a founder of quantum mechanics, once said, "How wonderful that we have met with a paradox. Now we have some hope of making progress" (Petersen, 1963). Bohr was fascinated by the idea of opposing truths (his self-designed coat of arms featured the motto *contraria sunt complementa*: "opposites are complementary"), and he was equally fascinated by language, remarking, "What is it that we human beings ultimately depend on? We depend on our words. We are suspended in language." *Intent/impact* and *both/and* are words to depend upon to keep understanding and progress in motion.

## Introducing This Language

There are many ways to introduce both/and language: in the context of a read-aloud, as a morning-meeting or closing-circle discussion question, or by shaping this language around a paradox in your classroom that you'd like to explore. (A kindergarten teacher might say, "It is both true that we are an affectionate, loving community and that it's important to ask a classmate's permission before hugging them.") Below, I model how you might introduce both/and language in the context of a closing-circle discussion.

Try a version of this:

**MS. LILY:** Before we all head home today, I'm going to leave you with a snippet of language to mull over: "both/and," or the idea that contradictory things can be true at the same time. Both/and thinking is the opposite of either/or thinking, which is often an oversimplified way of considering things. Let's imagine that an older brother snatches a pencil out of your hand, and you feel incredibly frustrated, so you push him. In this moment, it is both true that your brother shouldn't have snatched your pencil *and* that it was wrong to push him.

The ability to respect multiple truths is like a superpower. Thinking this way unlocks all sorts of epiphanies you'd miss if you only stuck to either/or thinking. Think about your own life: What are two opposing truths that exist alongside each other? *It is both true that \_\_ and that \_\_.* For example, a former student once told me, "It is both true that I love my baby brother so much and that I want to put him in a box and mail him away sometimes."

**ELOISE:** It is both true that I love reading and that sometimes I'd rather just play and not have everyone ask me where my book is.

**MS. LILY:** Thank you for sharing. I think it's wonderful that you love reading *and* playing. We'll be using both/and language all year, and when you find yourself drifting toward either/or thinking (*I can only do \_\_, or Everyone thinks \_\_*), ask yourself: *Is there another truth here to discover?*

I typically share intent/impact language with kids in second grade and up a few days after introducing both/and language. I explain that intent/impact language helps us explore a specific kind of both/and thinking: Sometimes, what someone *means to do* and what they *actually do* are both true things that exist in opposition to each other. You might consider introducing this language alongside the Character Intent vs. Character Impact Reading Response in Curricular Connections, page 120.

## Kids' Turn

Here are some ways children can use and internalize this language.

- In the context of discussing literature:

    **ELI:** I think it's both true that Gerald [from Mo Willems's Elephant & Piggie series] is a little annoyed that Piggie won't give up her foolish flying ideas and that he likes how determined and funny she is.

- As older students explore the nuances of historical figures:

    **SYBIL:** I think it's both true that Alexander Hamilton believed in the cause of the Revolution and that he believed that America definitely shouldn't really be governed "by the people."

    **LUNA:** Gavrilo Princip's intent was to increase Serbian power in the Balkans by assassinating the Archduke, but his impact was . . . not that. He pretty much single-handedly triggered a series of events that led to World War I!

- In the context of an apology:

    **BOBBIE:** My intent was to just get my coat quickly, but my impact was that I elbowed you. I'm really, really sorry about that!

A gift of intent/impact language is that it empowers children to take responsibility for their actions while also maintaining their truth about their intentions (which, in turn, makes taking responsibility easier to bear).

# Curricular Connections

Apply the language across subject areas with these ideas.

**Reading Response: Character Intent vs. Character Impact**

This reading response helps older students consider the gulf between a character's intent and their impact. See page 143 for a reproducible template.

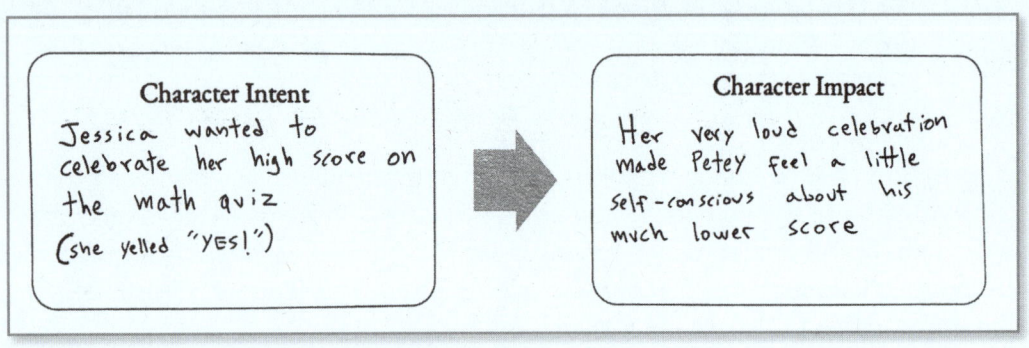

> **Character Intent**
> Jessica wanted to celebrate her high score on the math quiz (she yelled "YES!")
>
> ➡️
>
> **Character Impact**
> Her very loud celebration made Petey feel a little self-conscious about his much lower score

I jot down a student's analysis of a character's intent and impact.

**Poetry Invitation: Many Sides of Me**

Elementary schoolers are in the throes of figuring out who they are at school—the funny one? The smart one? The athletic one? The mischievous one? They are listening closely to how their teachers and peers talk about them and are finely attuned to what elicits praise or criticism. Throughout these tender and impressionable years, kids are especially susceptible to bucketing themselves in particular roles. Inviting children to write "Many Sides of Me" identity poems, inspired by both/and language, empowers them to resist categorization.

My student Quinn, an incredibly bright, kind child, was described by many classmates and teachers as the "the perfect student." But he was more than that; he was also creative, rambunctious, and silly. His outside-of-school friends saw this silly side, but not all of them knew about his intellectual strengths. In his poem, "The Two S's: Smart and Silly," on the right, Quinn writes about how special it is to be able to show his *full self* to others.

> **The Two S's: Smart and Silly**
> by Quinn
>
> some people
> think that
> I'm smart
> but don't
> know I'm
> silly
>
> some people
> think that
> I'm silly
> but don't
> know I'm
> smart
>
> some people
> know that
> I'm both
> and appreciate
> me for
> it
>
> they are my true
> friends
>
> who I dare
> show
> both sides
> of me
> to.

The Words That Shape Us

# Partnering With Families

Share these strategies with families for weaving the language into their home lives.

**Parents can use intent/impact language to help children understand the consequences of their choices.**

PARENT: I believe that your intent was to simply express excitement about Julia's birthday party. But because not every child is invited, the impact of talking about it at school is that some kids may feel left out.

**Family members can use both/and language to write "Many Sides of Me" poems alongside their children.**

> I am both Cuban and American
> I am both your mother and my mother's little one
>
> At the end of the day
> I am tired
> And
> I am so happy
> To be singing with you.

> **I am both a country mouse and a city mouse**
>
> I love a praying mantis and I love a croissant
> A tractor's grumble-rumble and a siren's wail
> The sacred aloneness and possibility of a just-mowed field
> The buzz and heat and cinnamon-y scent of a packed coffee shop
> Constellations of blueberry muffin crumbs below tiny Velcro-ed feet.

# Conclusion

There are moments in the classroom—moments like Leo's "mirror" share or Charlotte's "important thing" tribute to Eleanor—that pierce the familiar routines of the school day and feel sacred. Time slows down, and something shifts within you or within the student. Most of the time, growth is incremental. Once in a while, it bowls you over.

A third moment like this occurred a few years ago at our classroom poetry café. After the children read aloud their original poems, Anneliese and I asked the parents in the audience if anyone might volunteer to read a poem that they loved. Rachel, a writer and teacher, stepped up to the microphone and into the brightness of the jury-rigged spotlight we had attached to the ceiling. Holding her 3-year-old son Max's hand, she unfolded a piece of paper and read an excerpt from Kahlil Gibran's "On Children":

> **On Children**
> by Kahlil Gibran
>
> Your children are not your children.
> They are the sons and the daughters of Life's longing for itself.
> They come through you but not from you,
> And though they are with you yet they belong not to you.
>
> You may give them your love but not your thoughts,
> For they have their own thoughts.
> You may house their bodies but not their souls,
> For their souls dwell in the house of tomorrow,
> Which you cannot visit, not even in your dreams.

Rachel's chin trembled, and so did her right hand holding the poem. Her outstretched left hand, the one Max's little fingers were wrapped around, was as steady as can be. Max stood confidently beside his mother and looked right out at the audience. Together, the two of them embodied Gibran's words: Rachel was *with* her child but not *in charge* of him, loving her child while also celebrating his inherent separateness from her.

As I looked at Rachel and Max and listened to "On Children" for the very first time, I felt that rare inner shifting. Not yet a parent, I thought of the children in my care: *My students are not my students.* They don't belong to the school, the classroom, the curriculum—they belong to themselves. It's not my job to give them my prepackaged thoughts. But I can give them words; words that open doors to their own new, beautiful thoughts. Thoughts that empower them to trust themselves, take risks, and look for nuance all around them.

Teaching elementary school is a mysterious profession in that our influence is often invisible.

Middle school-, high school-, and college-aged students have the independence and technology to send an email to recent or current teachers, and these check-ins can feel like "proof" of impact. By contrast, young children enter our classrooms and then leave them, and they often don't have the information to contact us later even if they wanted to. But I hope that, as an elementary school educator, you won't forget that you have a secret power. You are a trusted grown-up in one of the most formative moments in your students' lives; a moment when their capacity for neuroplasticity is extraordinary and their sense of self is rapidly evolving. The words you share can literally shape how their brains receive information and predict, transforming how they think, feel, and behave—now *and* later.

Twenty years from now, a student from your second-grade class may remember to think ishfully and keep perfectionism at bay so she can finally begin a long-deferred endeavor. Or go bird by bird, doing the next small right thing in front of her as she moves forward after a shattering loss. Or listen to her wisest self and make the difficult-but-kind choice when others around her aren't. You, and the language you shared, cross space and time to become a part of those moments. Writer Anthony Doerr (2014) compares the air around us to a library: "every sentence spoken, every word transmitted still reverberating within it." The words you share with your students will reverberate, on and on, in ways you can never know.

# Acknowledgments

Ann Patchett says that to write a book, authors must "be willing to break our own hearts by trading in the living beauty of imagination for the stark disappointment of words." I relate to this. Although this is a book about the power of words, I feared I wouldn't be able to find the right ones. So I held tight to my imaginary book and dreamed up excuses to avoid getting started on the real one.

Wendy Murray is the person who finally got me writing. Our conversation about language in early 2023 motivated me to sit down, stare at my computer screen, type a few sentences, and see what happened next. I am forever indebted to you, Wendy.

To the Scholastic team: Sarah Longhi and Ray Coutu, your initial encouragement and feedback helped bring these ideas to life. Maria Chang, your immediate belief in and advocacy for this book brought it across the finish line. Thank you for your flexibility and wisdom throughout the editing process, and for reminding me to take things bird by bird. Tannaz Fassihi and Maria Lilja, I am so grateful for your gorgeous cover and interior page designs. Bobby McCabe, thank you for working hard to bring this book to readers. Tara Welty, thank you for your faith in teachers and your commitment to elevating our voices.

My deepest thanks to my former students: Your genius and open-heartedness infused each school day with wonder, and your contributions are the best parts of this book. To the parents of each of my former students: Thank you for trusting me to care for your whole world, your hearts.

To my most recent partner teachers—Casey Carlson and Anneliese Rosen—delighting in the kids next to you was one of my favorite parts of the job. To my colleagues, teachers, and mentors over the years, thank you for your inspiration and guidance. A few of the wonderful educators who informed ideas central to this book are Sara Despres, Liz Phillips, Beth Handman, Dana Rappaport, Gravity Goldberg, Dana Clark, Heather Frank, Brianne Anitti, Lynne Einbender, Sean O' Shea, Judith Leipzig, Debbie Niderberg, Sara Diament, Claire Wurtzel, Randall Flinn, Susan Sterman-Jones, Elizabeth Abrams, Andrew Ritsema, Carol Collet, Craig Smith, Andy Reyes, Rives Collins, Drew and Anne Mackay, Kate Davis, Jessica Gillespie, Elizabeth Eastwick, Maddie Fromell, Marcus Sesin, Carolyn Hammonds, Carissa Youse, Theresa Luongo, Emily Taylor, and Kevin Murawski. Thank you especially to Andrea Rousso, who introduced me to Ross Greene's work and who taught me to always interpret hard moments—with kids *and* grown-ups—in the most charitable light. To Georgia Heard: Thank you for your beautiful foreword and for *Awakening the Heart: Exploring Poetry in Elementary and Middle School*, the book that has influenced me most as a teacher. You taught me that poetry can be a doorway to children's interior worlds; that it can empower kids with a capacity for introspection that will serve them for the rest of their lives.

To Rebecca Leighton and the teachers at Grace Church School in Brooklyn: Thank you for broadening my own children's circle of care and inspiring them to happily bounce into their preschool classrooms each morning. Because I knew my sons felt such warmth and belonging away from home, I felt peaceful focusing on this book. And thank you to the imaginative and loving Glenda Rice, the boys' favorite playmate and my dear friend. I could not have written this book without you.

To my father, Philip K. Howard: Thank you for showing me what it looks like to be brave, to take a shot at something, to work hard. To my mother, Alexandra Howard: Thank you for filling me up with so much love, presence, and joyful, responsive care that I knew to look for these gifts in other relationships. To my sisters, Charlotte Howard and Olivia Howard: Thank you for your steadfast encouragement and for hosting cousin playdates so I could buckle down and draft. To my brilliant wordsmith of a twin brother, Alexander Howard: Thank you for reveling in made-up language with me.

To my husband, Conrad Scott: The best thing that has ever happened to me was meeting you. You are the person I always want to talk to, improvise a poem with, notice the world next to. Thank you for teaching me how to have a birder mindset and pay attention to pigeons, rocks, the East River, everything. You have "opened up my eyes, taught me how to see, notice every tree," as Stephen Sondheim puts it. Thank you, also, for being my first reader and for managing the unheard-of: offering feedback in such a specific, diplomatic way that I found it impossible to respond defensively (most of the time).

And to my children, Alexander and Charlie: Your wisdom, capacity for silliness, and luminous, tender goodness takes my breath away. Listening to you shape words around your ideas and getting to know new parts of you each day is the joy of my life. To borrow language you taught me: I love you from the center of the center of my heart.

# References

Alko, S. (2015). *The case for Loving: The fight for interracial marriage*. Arthur A. Levine.

American Academy of Pediatrics. (2021). AAP-AACAP-CHA declaration of a national emergency in child and adolescent mental health. https://www.aap.org/en/advocacy/child-and-adolescent-healthy-mental-development/aap-aacap-cha-declaration-of-a-national-emergency-in-child-and-adolescent-mental-health/

Arnsten, A. F. (2015). Stress weakens prefrontal networks: Molecular insights to higher cognition. *Nature Neuroscience, 18*(10), 1376–1385. https://doi.org/10.1038/nn.4087

Barks, C. (2004). *The essential Rumi*. HarperOne.

Barrett, L. F. (2017, December). You aren't at the mercy of your emotions—your brain creates them [Video]. TED Conferences. https://www.ted.com/talks/lisa_feldman_barrett_you_aren_t_at_the_mercy_of_your_emotions_your_brain_creates_them

Barrett, L. F. (2017). *How emotions are made: the secret life of the brain*. Harper.

Barrett, L. F. (2020). People's words and actions can actually shape your brain—a neuroscientist explains how. TED Ideas. https://ideas.ted.com/peoples-words-and-actions-can-actually-shape-your-brain-a-neuroscientist-explains-how/

Bender, K. E. (2013, January 27). The accidental writer. *The New York Times*. https://www.nytimes.com/2013/01/27/books/review/the-accidental-writer.html

Bishop, R. S. (1990). Mirrors, windows, and sliding glass doors. *Collected perspectives: Choosing and using books for the classroom, 6*(3), 9–11. Christopher-Gordon Publishers.

Blackall, S. (2018). *Hello lighthouse*. Little, Brown.

Bomer, K. (2010). *Hidden gems: Naming and teaching from the brilliance in every student's writing*. Heinemann.

Brackett, M. (2019). *Permission to feel: Unlocking the power of emotions to help our kids, ourselves, and our society thrive*. Celadon Books.

Brown, B. (2018). *Dare to lead: Brave work. Tough conversations. Whole hearts*. Random House.

Brown, B. (2021). *Atlas of the heart: Mapping meaningful connection and the language of human experience*. Random House.

Brown, M. W. (1949). *The important book*. Harper & Bros.

Bryson, T. P., & Siegel, D. (2012). *The whole-brain child: 12 revolutionary strategies to nurture your child's developing mind*. Random House.

Cabrera, C. A. (2020). *Me & Mama*. Simon & Schuster.

Callard, A. (2019). Parenting and panic. *The Point Magazine*.

Campbell, M. (2018). *Adrian Simcox does NOT have a horse*. Dial Books.

Centers for Disease Control and Prevention. (2017). Early brain development and health. https://archive.cdc.gov/www_cdc_gov/ncbddd/childdevelopment/early-brain-development.html

Christakis, E. (2016). *The importance of being little: What young children really need from grownups*. Penguin Books.

Curran, T. (2023). *The perfection trap: Embracing the power of good enough*. Scribner.

David, S. (2016). *Emotional agility: Get unstuck, embrace change, and thrive in work and life*. Avery.

DeAngelis, T. (2022). Anxiety among kids is on the rise. Wider access to CBT may provide needed solutions. *Monitor on Psychology, 53*(7), 38–42.

Doerr, A. (2014). *All the light we cannot see*. Scribner.

Doyle, G. (Host). (2021–present). We can do hard things [Audio podcast]. https://wecandohardthingspodcast.com

Dunn, J. (1983). Sibling relationships in early childhood. *Child Development, 54*(4), 787–811. https://www.jstor.org/stable/1129886

Dweck, C. S. (2007). *Mindset: The new psychology of success*. Ballantine Books.

Elbow, P. (2008). The believing game—Methodological believing. *English Department Faculty Publication Series, Paper 5*. http://scholarworks.umass.edu/eng_faculty_pubs/5

Estes, E. (1944). *The hundred dresses*. Harcourt, Brace & Company.

Fletcher, R. (2000). *How writers work: Finding a process that works for you*. HarperCollins.

Gay, R. (2019). *The book of delights: Essays*. Algonquin Books of Chapel Hill.

Gibran, K. (1923/2020). *The prophet*. Alfred A. Knopf.

Gibson, A. [@andreagibson]. (2019, January 13). There is so much love / in consistently asking … [Post]. X. https://x.com/andreagibson/status/1084652809700532228

Gilman, P. (2011). *The anti-romantic child: A memoir of unexpected joy*. HarperCollins.

Ginott, H. (1972). *Teacher and child: A book for parents and teachers*. Macmillan Company.

Gleitman, L., & Papafragou, A. (2012). New perspectives on language and thought. In K. J. Holyoak & R. G. Morrison (Eds.), *The Oxford handbook of thinking and reasoning* (pp. 543–568). Oxford University Press.

Greene, R. (2014). *Lost at school: Why our kids with behavioral challenges are falling through the cracks and how we can help them*. Scribner.

Greene, R. (2017). *Raising human beings: Creating a collaborative partnership with your child*. Scribner.

Haidt, J. (2024). *The anxious generation: How the great rewiring of childhood is causing a mental health epidemic*. Penguin Press.

Haughton, C. (2014). *Oh no, George!* Walker Books Ltd.

Heard, G. (1999). *Awakening the heart: Exploring poetry in elementary and middle school*. Heinemann.

Heard, G. (2009). *Falling down the page: A book of list poems*. Roaring Brook Press.

Heard, G. (2016). *Heart maps: Helping students create and craft authentic writing*. Heinemann.

Herschberg, R. (2024). It's impossible to raise a child who… [Instagram graphic]. https://www.instagram.com/rebeccahershbergphd/related_profiles/?hl=en

Howard, J. (1963, May 24). Telling talk from a Negro writer. *LIFE, 54*(21), 81.

Immordino-Yang, M. H. (2015). *Emotions, learning, and the brain: Exploring the educational implications of affective neuroscience*. W.W. Norton & Company.

John, J. (2018). *The bad seed*. HarperCollins.

Jones, C. F. (1991). *Mistakes that worked: 40 familiar inventions & how they came to be*. Delacorte Press.

Kahneman, D. (2013). *Thinking, fast and slow*. Farrar, Straus and Giroux.

Kennedy, B. (2022). *Good inside: A guide to becoming the parent you want to be*. HarperCollins.

Kennedy, B. (2023 April). The single most important parenting strategy [Video]. TED Conferences. https://www.ted.com/talks/becky_kennedy_the_single_most_important_parenting_strategy

Kim, A. (2023). *Happiness falls*. Hogarth.

Klein, E. (Host). (2021, February 19). What it means to be kind in a cruel world [Audio podcast episode]. *The Ezra Klein Show*. *The New York Times*. https://www.nytimes.com/2021/02/19/opinion/ezra-klein-podcast-george-saunders.html

Klein, E. (Host). (2024, March 5). Marilynne Robinson on biblical beauty, human evil, and the idea of Israel [Audio podcast episode]. The Ezra Klein Show. *The New York Times*. https://www.nytimes.com/2024/03/05/podcasts/transcript-ezra-klein-interviews-marilynne-robinson.html

Lamott, A. (1995). *Bird by bird: Some instructions on writing and life*. Vintage.

Levy, D. (2016). *I dissent: Ruth Bader Ginsburg makes her mark*. Simon & Schuster.

Lin, G. (2018). *A big mooncake for little star*. Little, Brown.

Lindquist, K. A., Satpute, A. B., & Gendron, M. (2015). Does language do more than communicate emotion? *Current Directions in Psychological Science, 24*(2), 99–108.

MacFarquhar, L. (2018, March 26). The mind-expanding ideas of Andy Clark. *The New Yorker*. https://www.newyorker.com/magazine/2018/04/02/the-mind-expanding-ideas-of-andy-clark

Mark, G. (2023). *Attention span: A groundbreaking way to restore balance, happiness, and productivity*. Hanover Square Press.

Moore, R. (1966). *Niels Bohr: The man, his science, and the world they changed*. Alfred A. Knopf.

Muhammad, G. (2020). *Cultivating genius: An equity framework for culturally and historically responsive literacy*. Scholastic.

Muller, J. Z. (2018). *The tyranny of metrics*. Princeton University Press.

Murthy, V. (2023). Social media and youth mental health: The U.S. Surgeon General's advisory. U.S. Department of Health and Human Services. https://www.hhs.gov/sites/default/files/sg-youth-mental-health-social-media-advisory.pdf

Nelson, M. (2015). *The argonauts*. Graywolf Press.

Oliver, M. (2017). *Devotions: The selected poems of Mary Oliver*. Penguin Books.

Palmer, P. J. (2007). *The courage to teach: Exploring the inner landscape of a teacher's life*. Jossey-Bass.

Patchett, A. (2013). *This is the story of a happy marriage*. HarperCollins.

Perel, E. (Host). (2017–present). *Where should we begin?* [Audio podcast]. Audible. https://www.audible.com/pd/Where-Should-We-Begin

Perry, B. D., & Winfrey, O. (2021). *What happened to you? Conversations on trauma, resilience, and healing*. Flatiron Books.

Petersen, A. (1963). The philosophy of Niels Bohr. *Bulletin of the Atomic Scientists, 19*(7), 8–14. https://doi.org/10.1080/00963402.1963.11454520

Reynolds, P. H. (2004). *Ish*. Candlewick Press.

Rosenthal, A. K. (2006). *One of those days*. G. P. Putnam's Sons Books for Young Readers.

Ruhl, S., & Ritvo, M. (2018). *Letters from Max: A poet, a teacher, a friendship*. Milkweed Editions.

Ruiz, D. M. (1997). *The four agreements: A practical guide to personal freedom*. Amber-Allen Publishing.

Sapolsky, R. M. (2017). *Behave: The biology of humans at our best and worst*. Penguin Press.

Schnall, S., Haidt, J., Clore, G. L., & Jordan, A. H. (2008). Disgust as embodied moral judgment. *Personality and Social Psychology Bulletin, 34*(8), 1096–1109. https://doi.org/10.1177/0146167208317771

Schwartz, R. (2021). *No bad parts: Healing trauma & restoring wholeness with the internal family systems model*. Sounds True.

Silverman, E. (2018). *Jack (not Jackie)*. Little Bee Books.

Smith, W. K. & Lewis, M. W. (2022). *Both/and thinking: Embracing creative tensions to solve your toughest problems*. Harvard Business Review Press.

Sondheim, S. (1984). *Sunday in the Park with George*. Original Broadway Cast.

Soo, P., & Pasquale Doran, M. (2024). *Piper Chen sings*. Penguin Random House.

Style, E. (1988). Curriculum as window and mirror. *Listening for All Voices*, Oak Knoll School monograph. https://www.nationalseedproject.org/Key-SEED-Texts/curriculum-as-window-and-mirror

Tabibnia, G., Lieberman, M. D., & Craske, M. G. (2008). The lasting effect of words on feelings: Words may facilitate exposure effects to threatening images. *Emotion, 8*(3), 307–317. https://doi.org/10.1037/1528-3542.8.3.307

Tippett, K. (Host). (2015, February 5). Mary Oliver: I got saved by the beauty of the world [Audio podcast]. On Being with Krista Tippett. https://onbeing.org/programs/mary-oliver-i-got-saved-by-the-beauty-of-the-world/

Tolstoy, L. (2004). *Anna Karenina* (R. Pevear & L. Volokhonsky, Trans.). Penguin Books. (Original work published 1877).

Wallace, D. F. (2009). *This is water: Some thoughts, delivered on a significant occasion, about living a compassionate life*. Little, Brown and Company.

Walsh, C. (2018, July 6). For Marilynne Robinson, literary explorer, gifts of language reward journey. *The Harvard Gazette*. https://news.harvard.edu/gazette/story/2018/07/in-visit-to-harvard-marilynne-robinson-discusses-teaching-writing/

Whyte, D. (2021). *Consolations: The solace, nourishment, and underlying meaning of everyday words*. Many Rivers Press.

Willems, M. (2007). *Today I will fly!* Hyperion Books.

Williams, V. B. (1982). *A chair for my mother*. Greenwillow Books.

Woodson, J. (2010). *Each kindness*. Nancy Paulsen Books.

Wu, T. (2016). *The attention merchants: The epic scramble to get inside our heads*. Vintage Books.

Yeager, D. S., Hanselman, P., Walton, G. M. et al. (2019). A national experiment reveals where a growth mindset improves achievement. *Nature 573*, 364–369 https://doi.org/10.1038/s41586-019-1466-y

Zander, R. S. & Zander, B. (2002). *The art of possibility: Transforming professional and personal life*. Penguin Books.

# Appendix: Reproducible Templates

Outer Shell/Inner Swirls Identity Map ................................................. 130

Reading Response: Outer Shell/Inner Swirls Character Map ............... 131

Reading Response: Interrupting Assumptions .................................... 132

More Mirrors, Please! ........................................................................ 133

"Important Thing" Planner ................................................................. 134

Reading Response: Coaching Characters ........................................... 135

Switch on Your Birder Mindset .......................................................... 136

What Will You Notice? ....................................................................... 137

Brilliant Mistakes Lead to Brilliant Learning ...................................... 139

Ishfully Dream Ideas Into Being ......................................................... 140

Reading Response: Beyond "Traits" ................................................... 141

Reading Response: Beneath Behavior ............................................... 142

Reading Response: Character Intent vs. Character Impact ............... 143

Name: _____   Date: _____

# Outer Shell/Inner Swirls Identity Map

Name: _____ Date: _____

# Reading Response: Outer Shell/Inner Swirls Character Map

Book: _____

Character: _____

Name: _____ Date: _____

# Reading Response: Interrupting Assumptions

Book: _____ Character: _____

- Assumption
- Information That Disrupts Assumption
- Deeper Understanding: Just because …

*The Words That Shape Us: The Science-Based Power of Teacher Language* © by Lily Howard Scott, Scholastic Teaching Solutions • page 132

Name: _____  Date: _____

# More Mirrors, Please!

I think there should be more mirrors in books and media for:
_____

**Why?**

_____
_____
_____
_____
_____
_____
_____
_____
_____
_____
_____
_____
_____

Name: _____  Date: _____

# "Important Thing" Planner

Think about this person's idiosyncrasies, interests, and strengths.
How can you make them feel truly known and celebrated?

_____,
(Person's name)


To me, an important thing about you is _____

_____.


It is true that you _____

_____.


It is true that you _____

_____.


It is true that you _____

_____.


But to me, an important thing about you is _____

_____.

Name: _____  Date: _____

# Reading Response: Coaching Characters

Book: _____

Character: _____

| Character's emotional experience | Imagine yourself as this character's wisest self: *What would you say?* |
|---|---|
| Character's emotional experience | Imagine yourself as this character's wisest self: *What would you say?* |

Name: _____  Date: _____

# Switch on Your Birder Mindset

We find what we look for. What funny, joyful, odd, interesting thing will you notice?

| I see . . . | I hear . . . |
|---|---|
| | |

| I wonder . . . | I am amused by . . . |
|---|---|
| | |

# What will you notice?

_____
_____
_____
_____
_____
_____

8

_____
_____
_____
_____
_____
_____

1

_____
_____
_____
_____
_____
_____

6

_____
_____
_____
_____
_____
_____

3

2

_____
_____
_____
_____
_____
_____

7

_____
_____
_____
_____
_____
_____

4

_____
_____
_____
_____
_____
_____

5

_____
_____
_____
_____
_____
_____

Name: _____  Date: _____

# Brilliant Mistakes Lead to Brilliant Learning

| Mistake (Oops!) | Learning 💡 |
|---|---|
| | |

Name: _____  Date: _____

# Ishfully Dream Ideas Into Being

Think of your pencil as containing magic your head doesn't know about yet. Choose the first idea that pops into your mind and don't judge it—just go!

**Think of an animal. What is it?** _____

**Think of another animal. What is it?** _____

Now, imagine a creature that is a combination of these two animals. Quickly name and sketch the creature.

**Creature's name:**

_____

**What is this creature's personality like?**

| Likes | Dislikes |
|---|---|
|  |  |

Name: _____ Date: _____

# Reading Response: Beyond "Traits"

Book: _____

Character: _____

**Respond to four questions that resonate with you.**

| What wonderings do you have about this character? | Any theories about what might drive some of this character's behavior? |
|---|---|
| What are some good choices that this character makes? | What are some bad choices that this character makes? |
| What is something this character is working on? | What is something you admire about this character? |

Name: _____ Date: _____

# Reading Response: Beneath Behavior

Book: _____

Character: _____

| What are some things that are uniquely hard for this character? | How are these "hard things" connected to their choices? |
|---|---|
|  |  |
|  |  |

Name: _____  Date: _____

# Reading Response:
# Character Intent vs. Character Impact

Book: _____

Character: _____

| Character Intent | ➡ | Character Impact |
|---|---|---|
| | | |

# Notes